A Marvelous Paranoia

A Memoir

Terry Simons

RBP

Copyright 2010 Round Bend Press

Published by
Round Bend Press
1115 S.W. 11th Avenue Suite 401
Portland, OR 97205

First Edition

ISBN: 978-0-9831840-0-3

roundbendpress@yahoo.com
roundbendpress.blogspot.com

Other books by the author:

Fiction

The Friends of Round Bend (A Novel)
Two Stories:
(How Bees Carry Forth the Essence of Man's Faith in One
Omniscient God & The Soldier)

Plays

Litany in a Trumpeter's Bog
The Opening
The Law of Revenge
The Problem
Two Plays

Essays

Alt-Everything
Of Dirty Kitchens, Bedlam & the Bomb

Screenplays

The Friends of Round Bend
Red Green & Yellow

Graphic Art

Yes, But You Don't Understand!

Author's Note

This is a memoir. The names of several people from my past have been changed to protect their innocence. The small Oregon town where I grew up is Sweet Home. When I lived there from 1951 to 1969, Sweet Home was a logging and lumber community. Today the town's biggest enterprises are tourism and a country music festival held yearly in the summer. The times they did change.

The years remembered in this book, with a few exceptions, are 1951 to 1980. The conversations quoted herein are reasonable approximations of actual conversations that occurred many years ago. They are truthful to the spirit of memory.

Additionally, I want to thank K.C. Bacon for reading the manuscript of this book and offering many suggestions for improving it.

Dedication

This one is for my daughter Stella and her son Dylan—my
sources of inspiration.

A writer is not so much someone who has something to say as he is someone who has found a process that will bring about new things he would not have thought of if he had not started to say them.

William Stafford

Steel Bridges

Portland, Oregon inspired me from an early age. For a kid growing up in a rural environment at the edge of the great Willamette Valley, the city represented irresistible mystery and an intoxicating vibrancy. When I visited my sister in Northwest Portland, I felt as if I was living inside a great adventure movie. I was the lead character, walking down the street with the camera following my every step. I was an actor in a serious movie about a youth and I might do something heroic in the next moment.

I enjoyed looking at the faces of strangers—an old man walking with a cane. He smiled and put me at ease. Women dressed differently than the women I watched in my home town. People acted differently than the people I knew. I didn't know what to make of these strangers. How could I begin to interpret what made them so different? I was a youngster. I didn't know anything about adulthood or the lives of others. All I could do is feel the city's life and absorb the newness that surrounded me. Its energy gave me a sense of joy and wonderment—a new view.

The city's architecture dazzled me with its mixture of tall, glass structures and old buildings crafted from brick and mortar. Colors leaped out at me as I walked through my sister's neighborhood. I discovered parks unlike any I had ever seen. They were a lush green, manicured, and labyrinthine. The great trees were different than the pine and fir in the woods near my home, though there were plenty of those, too. What did I know about the variety of trees and plants? Nothing! What did I know except the Hardy Boys, *Boy's Life* and baseball? Nothing!

Most of all, Portland's bridges fascinated me. I learned there were eight of them in the city proper, huge and odd-looking, much different than the old, wooden-covered bridge I knew from my swimming hole on the South Santiam River. Portland's bridges were made of steel, twisted and formed in unique patterns, mazes of iron and wire. I once stood and watched the Hawthorne Bridge rise, its middle section elevating mysteriously above the Willamette River. How? I noticed the large windowed booth atop the bridge. I realized—someone is up there! Someone sits up there! That, I thought, would be a great place to spend the day, just watching things. Raising the bridge, looking out at the round bend of the river on the horizon, waiting for another boat to pass under the bridge on the way to—where? I learned that was someone's job. How great would that be? I instantly wanted to be a bridge tender!

Portland left indelible images after my first visits, but soon waned in my imagination. I still visited as a member of various sports teams on occasion, but I had other things on my mind. I grew into my teens with other concerns, family troubles, and the personal and self-centered inhibitions of growth. My youth was a stretch of worrying years, marked by growing resentments, an expanding view of the unfairness of life. I became reclusive and uncommunicative. In my first year of high school I was put back a year in my reading exercises. I could read, but not as well as the school's psychologists wanted me to read. The news of my inability surprised me. I could remember being ahead in my reading exercises while in grade school. Then, as a freshman, I was dropped into the "Blue Room," a special lab for readers. I was told I lacked comprehension skills.

I knew what had happened. I had become distracted by the madness in my home, "the takeover" I came to call it, of my home by my oldest brother's three sons. They had moved into the small house I shared with my mother and sabotaged its peacefulness with a seething surface violence that both frightened and angered me.

And just before the brothers arrived something else had happened, a great tragedy in my neighborhood. A fire in a house next door to mine had wiped out all but one member of a large family that I had come to know well. The effects of this tragedy on my psyche were devastating. For many months afterward I did not sleep at all at night as my mind replayed the fire and deaths of my friends. I slept at school or simply sleepwalked through my daily activities. Given the circumstances there was no real mystery why I had fallen behind.

Three Sisters

I grew up in a small town east of Oregon's Willamette Valley, flush against the foothills of the Cascade Mountains. From my backyard on clear days I could see three far-off peaks known as the Three Sisters. Early settlers in the region had named them *Faith, Hope,* and *Charity.* The Native Americans who inhabited the area before the arrival of the whites likely had their own names for them—names unaffiliated with Christian sentiments. In due time, the sentimental names wore off. Today the peaks are rather mundanely referred to as North, Middle and South. The name Three Sisters had metaphorical overtones as well, evoking the image of a family hanging together under duress—in their case the volcanic violence of the Pleistocene epoch of hundreds of thousands of years ago.

The peaks are among the highest in the Cascade Range and have long been a playground for climbers, hikers and campers. My family camped there when I was a kid, and I have great memories of those times. We hiked along mountain trails and swam in ice-cold high lakes, and we fished for trout and took row boats and canoes far enough offshore to earn the admonishment our beer-swilling elders, who gathered around the campfire and gossiped, laughing at things the children were uninterested in or did not understand.

At night we sprayed on bug repellant and slept on thin mats inside tents, telling stories and listening to the sound of fish jumping in the lake and the sound of tree limbs bending in the summer breeze—nature's sounds. Occasionally, a dog barked and a nearby camper shouted at it to shut up. An infant might begin to cry, or a sudden storm might sneak in on blackened clouds and drench our tents with rain and quickly turn the campsite into a quagmire of mud and pine needles.

My family gathered at my sister Lucille's house before sunup whenever we prepared to go camping. We packed our gear into two or three cars, depending on how many family members could get away for the weekend. My brother-in-law, Lucille's husband, Henry Hogan, owned a wood-paneled Jeep Wagoneer that held most of the camping gear which we packed up before going into the house to eat a big breakfast of bacon and eggs, with pancakes and French toast on the side, and with hash browns and toast if you wanted them. By the time the sun came up we were on the road and ascending into the mountains in the direction of the Three Sisters wilderness area.

Unfortunately, the camping trips ended too soon with the early death of Henry Hogan. He was the family's camping and fishing guide, teacher and organizer, a great outdoorsman. He was also a deep-voiced country singer and an accomplished guitarist. I was about ten years-old when he died of Hodgkin's disease, at thirty-three. An Army veteran, he died in the Veterans Hospital in Portland, a terribly sad day for me because I truly loved the man. His five children worshipped him as well, of course, and his death crushed all of us. A brilliant and gifted man, he died way too young.

My sister Lucille was twenty-two years older than me and Henry had been a father figure. My father, Reuben, had died in an auto accident when I was six-months old. He was a logger like many other men in Oregon—a scaler, he weighed and measured logging truck loads as they descended from the mountains at Foster on the way to the mills. Driving home late one night, he crashed through a guardrail and into a deep ravine outside Cascadia, the tiny village in the lower Cascades where my family lived at the time. He survived the initial crash and climbed up the steep embankment before collapsing. A passing motorist found him the next morning. He was fifty-one, an age I believed quite old when I first heard the story.

My father's life was a brief interlude, I eventually realized. I am fifty-nine as I write this. I have lived nearly a decade longer than he did, and it seems like just yesterday that I too was a young man. Henry's and Reuben's lives were too short, but then all of our lives are too short. Everyone eventually realizes—some sooner than others—that humanity is guaranteed little, certainly not physical immortality.

The mountainous road where my father crashed was treacherous, with sheer drop-offs and tight corners, some of which didn't have guardrails. Improved and widened in recent years, in 1951 it represented a serious threat to all who traveled it. That stretch of road put the fear in me for years. I couldn't drive it without thinking about what had happened there to my father and to others.

At the time of my birth my family lived in a large, two-story house in Cascadia. It had a big front yard surrounded by a white-picket fence. A large willow tree stood in the front yard near one corner of the house, creating ample shade. I know, because there is a picture of me as an infant lying on my stomach on a blanket, staring at whoever was photographing me. The shade is covering my body; the edges of the blanket are blotched with sunlight. I look comfortable, at peace, wearing a sly grin.

The house sat adjacent to Cascadia State Park, known for its soda springs. I couldn't drink its acrid water, which was pumped from spigots at several locations throughout the park. I considered the water a highly acidic poison, but many in my family loved it. They claimed it had regenerative properties, and filled gallon jugs to take home and refrigerate. I could never get used to its smell and bitter bite, though I tried many times to develop a taste for the stuff, out of some sense of familial duty.

I don't remember living in the house in Cascadia. My mother moved the family down the mountain and closer to town shortly after my father's death. She didn't drive, so the move was absolutely necessary. Her kids—the ones old enough to drive—were long gone by then. Three of my brothers were in the Army in Korea at the time of my father's accident, and two of my sisters had families of their own. That left my brother Rich and sister Bethel at home with our mother and me in the big old house beside the park.

We moved down the mountain to Sweet Home—the larger nearby town where I was born—though itself little more than a small logging community. We visited the park and its environs often when I was young, passing through Cascadia on our trips to the high lakes. I can recall my mother's forlorn sighs whenever we visited the old place. I was young, but I think I understood at the time how wistful our circumstances made her feel. She shrunk with a tangible sadness when she gazed at the house. She and my father had lived there for most of their marriage of twenty-five years, so it must have, understandably, pained her to reflect on her memories of the place. Good and bad. Whatever she was thinking she never let on about it—around me at any rate.

Over the years the house began to rot away. I went up there years later and it was gone, but the big willow tree where I'd posed for my photo remained.

Lucille and her husband, Henry, had two kids of their own before I was born. My sister Evelyn had a son older than me, as did Lyle, the oldest of my four brothers. Those three siblings and my other brothers and sisters—seven in all— would keep pumping out the babies until there were too many to remember. I was already an uncle before I came out of the womb, a clear indication I was a dreadful mistake.

I grew up with my nieces and nephews, a nest of them born right around the same time I arrived, January 16, 1951. As we grew up together, attending the same schools, playing games, fighting, a few of them were more like brothers and sisters to me than my actual siblings. Though what actually happened was that I came to embrace solitude more than family. I was on my own a lot from a young age. My youngest sister, Bethel, was ten-years older than me. My youngest brother, Rich, was six-years older. Naturally, neither one of them wanted anything to do with me after they turned into teenagers.

Our age differences meant that by the time I turned twelve my mother and I were for one year alone in the house I grew up in at the end of Thompson Lane, which turned off Route 20 between Sweet Home and Foster. (Soon, unwanted company would join us, but for a brief time it was just my mother and me, our dog Buddy, and our four walls.)

When you are a twelve year-old boy you begin to lose interest in your mother, or at least I did. I figured out later that she was just as relieved to be done with me. Of dressing wounds and hearing the problems of children she'd had quite enough. She'd had enough by the time I turned that age— that is a certainty, and not just because of me, either. There were extenuating circumstances that influenced the whole of my teen years and my relationship to my mother.

Though we thrived for a short time alone, she enjoyed a sudden solitude when my brother left the house, finally, and I was glad to allow her the space she craved. We were capable of ignoring each other for days on end. We thrived on our unattached natures, and I enjoyed my solitude just as she enjoyed hers. I lived with the fantasies of which only a lonely child is capable or allowed, and I lived in a kind of secret dream world.

My twelfth year was perhaps the happiest year of my life. But the year was short and things would change soon enough.

Agriculture

I hated our routine. So did nearly every other sleepy-headed youngster living on Thompson Lane in the late fifties and throughout the sixties. Our parents made us rise early every weekday and most Saturdays from June to late August to go work in the fields.

"Get up," my mother would begin gently, tapping on the door of the bedroom I shared with my brother Rich. My eyes would blink open, and I thought, not again. Already? I'd look at my brother sleeping soundly next to me. He was six-years older and had learned how to tune out the ritualistic sound of our mother's voice. Five minutes might pass before she tapped again, a little harder this time. I prayed for rain. "I said get up!" she said. And again—yelling, "Get up or we'll miss the bus!" Fine, I thought. I'd like that. I'd like to have nothing to do today except play baseball or go fishing.

At my young age, our mother, Icie, might not have made me go into the fields with her to pick strawberries—I was too young to do any real work—except my brother didn't want to take care of me all day, and my youngest sister, Bethel, already had a social and work life that kept her preoccupied. She had a boyfriend and a job at a drive-in in town. I can't recall my brother ever going to the fields with us. My mother must have let him slide work-free in the interest of keeping the peace around the house.

I got up and ate a bowl of oatmeal while my mother prepared our lunches before we walked in the early-morning light out to Route 20 at the head of Thompson Lane. We crossed the highway and stood waiting for the beat up old retired school bus that Liggett Farms sent every morning from Lebanon on a fifty-mile round trip journey to gather the day's crew. The bus came into view every time, belching exhaust, rolling from the direction of Foster. My mother and I got on and took whatever seats were available.

I usually slept the entire fifteen-mile ride down from the foothills to the Farms outside Lebanon. The land flattens there, a portal to the Willamette Valley, and the fields stretch out like green and brown canvasses between the Coast Range and the Cascades.

This was agriculture. But at the tender age of six I couldn't pronounce the word, along with another word that amused me—linoleum.

In June we picked strawberries; rather my mother did. I bellyached, partly from eating too many strawberries, and roamed as far and wide through the fields as I could before my mother turned angry, telling me to sit next to her as she knelt in the soil. She picked and crated the fat red berries with hands that seemed to me to be running over the berry bushes like robotic claws.

I plucked a few more to eat. "Quit eating them!" my mother cried. I picked a few more and put them in her crate and

23

watched her take them to the station, where workers placed them carefully on flat-bed trucks. They stacked the crates to a legal height, which was too high, before driving off along the dusty road to the highway. The trucks always seemed to belch black and blue smoke, too, like the old bus.

A row boss punched my mother's ticket, indicating how many crates she'd picked. She grabbed another empty crate and came back, working from her haunches this time, donning her straw hat against the rising sun. I put my own straw hat on. The heat scorched down from the intensely blue sky, and I wished it would rain.

Eventually I was old enough to pick berries—in theory. But one day a row boss spoke to my mother. "Leave the kid at home," she suggested in a firm voice. "He slows you down, and he's not doing enough work. Mr. Liggett doesn't want kids out here who aren't working. Something could happen. They could get in trouble, or get hurt."

"Fine," my mother said, and I'd seen the last of the berry fields, though I tried picking raspberries for awhile one

A Marvelous Paranoia

summer, a tough way to make a buck because the smaller berries take forever to fill a crate.

At eight I began staying home alone in June as Icie went out to the strawberry fields by herself to earn a few dollars. She might haul in ten or fifteen dollars a day. In the evening with her red-stained crate tickets piled in front of her, she'd sit at the kitchen table, calculating her wages for the week. She counted twice, shook her head, and placed the tickets in an envelope for safe keeping.

I often occupied my time exploring the woods across the highway from Thompson Lane and fishing in the South Santiam River, and I discovered masturbation, growing quickly addicted to its sensations. I had a little girlfriend in the neighborhood. We went behind a logging truck garage owned by a neighbor and hid out, smoking unfiltered Camels and kissing. I got her to come into my house a few times alone with me. We kissed on my bed. I tried to touch her. "No," she said, but let me kiss her some more. Nine, ten, I was figuring things out for myself, like all perpetually horny young boys who experiment, trying to discover their emerging sexuality. A neighborhood boy and I got naked together and looked at each others privates. Our penises seemed huge and we laughed, but what could we do? We both liked girls, only we didn't know how to go about having sex with them. We were innocent, too young for sex, but curious. What the hell was sex, anyway? We were straight, and in the ensuing years we never talked about our adventure. Better to leave some things unsaid, I guess.

Every Friday my mother came home with a check. She cashed it at a grocery store in Foster. She'd bring me a magazine, a little ice-cream maybe. I don't recall her ever buying anything for herself, though she must have on occasion. She probably hid the stuff, keeping it under wraps in her bedroom—women's things. It was all very mysterious.

But then June passed and bush bean season started. I tried it for a short time, but it wasn't for me. Not in the slightest. My mother said, "Why won't you pick them? This is better than the berries. I can make better money here." And you could, but you still had to stoop over all day. I waited until the pole beans grew out a little later in the summer. I could actually make a little money then, as I got faster and faster later in the summer. I filled the five-gallon metal bucks we used with seeming ease. I'd race Icie to see which one of us could fill a bucket faster. She always won, but I was getting better. She'd reach deep into the vines and pull out a fistful. The beans seemed to align without effort in her hands; fat bunches of long beans that filled her bucket so quickly it astonished me. I worked hard just trying to keep up.

We filled burlap sacks to the brim. As I grew stronger I could hoist the heavy ones atop my shoulder, take them to the scalers and watch as a worker dumped the beans into large storage bins before punching my ticket. I brought in two-hundred pounds a day. Three, if I felt energetic. At four-cents a pound the money added up. I watched the jitney driver load the boxes on the flatbeds. It seemed to me that guy had the best job in the fields.

A row boss would walk along behind me briefly, picking the low beans I'd missed out of the dirt. I'd simply pause and stretch my back. "You've got to get these," she'd say, dropping the beans into my bucket. Then she pulled the vines back and spoke directly to my mother on the other side of the row. "Watch him," she said. "He's missing too many."

One summer the row boss was my high school baseball coach and PE teacher. Teachers always had to take summer jobs back then, especially if they had families. My teachers were always some of the best people I knew. Accordingly, I respected them. Later, I wondered why they were paid so little for doing such an important job. You see, I hadn't figured America out yet. Teachers' salaries have gone up in recent years; a good thing provided they are competent. But no elementary or high school teacher makes as much as a congressman, for instance, and the teacher is much more valuable in the big picture.

Liggett Farms hired a bus driver one summer who was always drunk at the end of the day. Driving home from the field, a fifteen mile journey in an unsafe bus, he swerved all over the road. The guy lasted the entire summer, until Mr. Liggett finally fired him. I dreaded the ride home from the fields that summer. Every day I expected the bus to crash, killing everyone. We did have many close calls as it turned out. Vehicle crashes played big in my imagination, probably because of the circumstances surrounding my father's death. I constructed fantasies of rollovers and people being hurled across the highway, victims, like my father, of speed and recklessness, of technology trumping humanity.

Summers worked like this for me throughout the sixties. If it rained, I didn't pick beans that day. If I had an afternoon baseball game, my mother let me do that rather than work. But the rest of the time I picked beans. I could make ten dollars a day. My mother could make twenty. One summer, I saved enough to buy my first bicycle and a pump-action BB gun. Within days I was one of the fastest riders in the neighborhood. Our races up and down Airport Road were fierce competitions. We raced from the airport to Route 20, about a half-mile along two lanes of blacktop. After awhile nobody could beat me.

Death on Thompson Lane

I awakened to the color of fire dancing in my bedroom window. With my brother in the Marines, I was alone in my room and heard voices, the terror of something awful in the darkness beyond the crimson light rubbing my widow pane. I got out of bed and hurried to the window, which looked out to the front yard and through the leaves of a large willow tree, and through the leaves I could see red and yellow flames shooting a hundred-feet into the black sky and the entire large two-story house next door engulfed in flames.

I thought I must be dreaming, but the terrified voices quickly convinced me otherwise. Neighbors were gathered outside as I looked through the window. Odd shapes, silhouetted forms were running in every direction like shadow puppets. In the distance I heard a fire alarm. It was coming from two miles away, the call to the volunteer fire department in town. Within moments I heard the sirens; firefighters were coming down the highway in our direction. A man ran toward the burning house. Another man grabbed him and shouted: "No! We can't get any closer! It's too hot!"

I felt the heat through the window pane now. I went outside. A crowd had gathered and people from all over the neighborhood were watching the fire. Kids and women were milling about, and hysteria gripped the scene—more shouting, broken-throated wailing, kids clinging to their mothers, terrified by what they were witnessing. Intense heat seared the night.

The fire trucks began to bounce down Thompson Lane, kicking up dust. A stream of vehicles rushed to the fire— volunteers arrived in their private cars and trucks. The men ran towards the house, throwing their fire gear on as they moved. I was close enough to hear them shouting. "The mother was out," one of them yelled to a new arrival. "She went back inside. I tried to stop her!" They talked. They were trying to figure out how many were in there. I looked at the fire and then at them again. They inched closer to the inferno, but the heat drove them back. They were helpless. I grew as terrified as everyone else, the smoke and heat attacking all of my senses.

The fire hoses finally came out and the men stood back and sprayed the raging fire with long arcs of water that seemed to fall without effect on the flames. The blaze had grown to immense proportions, and then a side of the house suddenly collapsed, sending sparks into the air like logs on a campfire. Suddenly I could see a man running fast up Thompson Lane from the highway. I recognized him. He lived in the house with his mother and six brother and sisters. He was screaming as he ran toward the house, getting as close to the fire as anyone I'd seen until then, but the heat drove even him back, staggering, and several firemen restrained him. He fought back hard, striding toward the fire, throwing his elbows at the firemen who had him locked down at the waist and shoulders.

He was Jim, the oldest sibling in the family, and he was the only one absent when the fire broke out at 3 a.m., sparked, they determined later, by a cocktail of oil and rags in a workshop attached to the house. Officials theorized that the summer heat had ignited the rags; others thought one of the kids had been smoking in the shop earlier in the day. I never heard whether they ever determined the absolute truth. The fire "experts" were, after all, only volunteers.

Apparently, the family slept while the fire quickly spread to the large front porch and entry to the house. Within moments it leaped into the interior, fingers of fire torching the first floor ceiling and racing up the stairwell. As the neighborhood slept, the roof was ablaze within minutes.

People had seen the mother outside and tried to stop her. But she returned to the inferno to try to save her children. When firefighters found her body—the parts of flesh that remained in the blackened ashes the next day—she lay near where the back door had been. Under her body searchers found her youngest, a six-year old boy with Down Syndrome. He had been relatively untouched by the flames. His mother had fallen with him and managed to blanket him with her body as they died.

The other bodies were scattered throughout the blackened ruins. There had been four bedrooms in the house. One was in the attic. Now the house was a flattened mass of charred lumber and concrete and smelled of smoldering timbers and ash—and death.

I'd come to know death intimately in a stunning and frightening moment. And I was traumatized by it. I'd known the family since it moved to Oregon from Utah the previous year. The mother was on her own, a divorcee. Her oldest son Jim worked in the woods and helped support the family. I ran in and out of their house like one of her middle sons, my playmates. I raced with them on Airport Road and we organized baseball games in the hay field behind my house, where we built huge forts of hay bales, maze-like structures that became secret hiding places. We hunted rats out of my woodpile, trapped them and hung them by their tails on the clothesline, finishing them off with BB shot, destroying the vulgar things.

I liked the oldest son, Jim. I respected him because he was tough but unthreatening. Word had it that he was at his girlfriend's house that morning before being notified of the fire. I don't know how he learned of it; perhaps he was close enough to hear it or see it. I always imagined if Jim had been home that night he would have saved them all. I didn't know this, of course, but I believed it because he was a man. He was twenty-one and tough, I could tell. He was a logger like many of the men in town. Like them, he was as tough as they come.

Also, a pretty, long-haired girl I'd fallen in love with died in the fire. I'd kissed her a few times that first summer and we liked each other. She taught me how to play cribbage on the front porch of that house, with her brothers and the little guy hanging around. She would playfully push the six year-old away and scold him for touching the cards as we played our hands. If two of her brothers decided to play we had a full game and would play long into the night. The mother brought Kool-Aid and sandwiches out to the porch. She fed me along with her brood, making it easy for my mom.

The fire set me back at least for a year, probably much longer. When school started a few weeks later I slept in class because each night brought the trauma home again in the dark of my quiet house. I lay in the bed I now had to myself, night after night, and anguished. I would smell the fire, unable to sleep. If I occasionally managed to doze, I always awoke with a start and a great throbbing fear that I could not explain to anyone. Not even to my mother, who must have known I was in agony but was powerless to help me. She could do nothing to help me sleep or alleviate the terror that paralyzed me every night.

The Takeover

The house on Thompson Lane was a humble home, my sanctuary, a place where my quiet mother and I retreated from the world and enjoyed our solitude. Both of us loved to read. Reading especially occupied our evenings once our old Zenith television died. My mother sat in her reading chair under a tall reading lamp and I retired to my bedroom, stretching out on the big bed I had once shared with my brother.

Before the television broke down we watched *Gunsmoke* together. But when the *Lawrence Welk Show* came on my mother had the television to herself. I could find plenty to do to avoid that awful music. I had music of my own and my transistor radio to listen to Wolfman Jack and Top 40 music and long-forgotten talk shows. I also had a stereo that I'd received for Christmas one year and a few Elvis and Gene Pitney records I could listen to. With luck I could catch the Giants broadcasts from Candlestick Park in San Francisco on my transistor while dreaming of playing there one day. But mainly, I had the solitude that I craved and needed.

When my mother and I were living alone together on Thompson Lane, Kennedy was assassinated in Dallas and we watched the report on our old Zenith before it crashed. A staunch Democrat, my mother took Kennedy's death hard, for she believed he was the second coming of FDR. I knew that Lincoln and McKinley had been assassinated, but that was history. How could anybody kill Kennedy? Death was too easy, I thought. So was fear.

When disaster stuck it kept piling on.

The home's burnt-out shell sat next door for months without anyone moving a finger to clean it up. It was a constant reminder of what had happened. I dreamed fire and death the whole time, and I went to school tired and slept the academic year away. Years later I realized I probably needed trauma counseling after the fire, but schools—or mine in any case—didn't do things that way when I was a youngster. But my teacher knew why I slept most of the day, and she kindly allowed me the opportunity without objection.

My happy childhood ended with the fire and its trauma. Soon another disaster that I had no control over further complicated my troubled adolescence.

This situation lasted for five long, dreadful years. I would be untruthful if I claimed its effects no longer matter or were completely eradicated. The psychological scars of these events are buried deep; I still feel them. They have lingered for years and etched my personality no less profoundly than the fire did. They eroded my remaining confidence and sense of inner joy. Mere degrees separate the turmoil in my life created by the deaths of my friends by fire and the lingering significance that I attach to what I called "the takeover."

My brother Lyle, the oldest sibling in our family and the one I barely knew, had fathered three boys, raising them in Reedsport on the Oregon coast. I knew he had worked for years as a log truck driver, but I didn't know my brother or his sons well at all, for they seldom came inland from the coast to visit. The boys were all clustered around my age. They were twelve, thirteen and fourteen when their parents' marriage collapsed and the family fell apart. I was never clear about what happened at the coast between Lyle and my nephews' mother, but it was clearly ruinous. The boys ended up on their grandmother's lap. My house!

The fire had been hellish, but things grew even more hellish with the arrival of Leroy, Carmen, and Steve. The first major problem I faced with this sudden rearrangement in my life was the boys' outrageous and at times uncontrollable anger. Looking back years later, I realized their parents' divorce had devastated them and contributed to their pathological meanness.

My own father had died when I was an infant, and I had no comprehension of what a father meant to a child or even really what family life entailed. My life had been defined early by not having a father and I had no choice in the matter. I was fine with that, though the older I got the more significant my loss seemed to me. Of course living without a father shaped my life as much as the fire and my nephews' sudden appearance had, but not particularly in any negative fashion. You don't miss what you've never known. My nephews missed their father and mother deeply, and my mother and I paid for that, as they did within the context of their own damaged psyches and their exploding resentment.

The oldest boy, Leroy, was sullen and tougher than anybody I knew. He loved to fight and he would fight at the slightest provocation. He would fight until his enemy begged forgiveness. He once knocked out a neighborhood kid named Freddy with one punch. I saw that one happen, a punch that seemed to come from nowhere, flattening poor Freddy. The kid had challenged Leroy and my nephew didn't hesitate to think about it, he just reacted with a punch, a quick right-cross that caught Freddy on the jaw. Down Freddy went from his heels, dropping straight back like a long board. Freddy hit his head on a dog bone when he struck the ground and he didn't wake up until his mother put a cold compress to his forehead and begged him to wake up.

I panicked when I saw that punch. I thought Freddy had been killed. It was a sucker punch, but Freddy had asked for it

Leroy was a good baseball player and had a great sense of humor when he wasn't angry, which wasn't often. Of the three brothers, he was in many ways the nicest and most even tempered. But when he erupted things got out of hand fast. He was the one brother you simply did not want to agitate. He was smart and quick to let you know it. And he hated idle talk. If you started a conversation with him, you'd best know what you were talking about and what you were trying to tell him. If you stumbled, he'd walk away and call you a name, leaving you to wonder what you'd done to offend him. He tortured his brothers all the time with this quirky aspect of his personality. I learned to stay clear of Leroy if I could, but in my small house we had our moments of near mayhem. Leroy had the brains in the family, and he was probably smart enough to know the situation was untenable and he perhaps even felt badly about intruding on my mother and me, though he never talked about it. Like all of us, he had no other option if he wanted to finish school before moving on.

The second nephew's name was Carmen, but he preferred his middle name, Leon. I despised this kid. He was a vain, self-centered greaser, and effeminate in a way that made him compensate by trying to be a tough guy all the time. He was also dumb, and had a dumb kid's look of incomprehension perpetually plastered to his face. Like his older brother, Carmen loved to fight, but he wasn't as adept at it as Leroy. He worshipped Leroy, but they fought like a pair of alley cats. For Leroy, Carmen was a pushover. A couple of solid blows and Carmen would quit. Then he'd go out and try someone else, someone he knew he could handle just to make himself feel better. The word punk wasn't used much then, like it is today, but if it was, someone would have called Carmen a punk.

Carmen and I never actually got into it physically, but when we spoke to each other a constant tension ate the room and threatened to erupt into violence. Carmen had a greaser friend named Todd throughout high school. Todd later died in a motorcycle accident, but when they were together the two greasers made sport of terrorizing others. They picked fights with chumps. Occasionally they picked the wrong chump and got the crap kicked out of them, which I always appreciated as justice served.

Steve was the youngest, a crybaby, and the most loving towards my mother—where any love at all was exhibited. He dropped out of high school and joined the Marines, in 1969. Later, he came back to our small town and told everyone he'd been wounded in Vietnam. Then he went over to my grandmother's house—his great grandmother—and stole all the cash she kept under her mattress. He'd seen her take the money out at various times to give small cash gifts to her many grandkids. Steve disappeared with the money and a Marine rep showed up in town soon thereafter looking for him. Steve had never been to Vietnam; he was AWOL and on the run.

The three boys crowded into my bedroom, with predictable results. I had to give my bed to two of them and my mom pulled a hide-a-bed out of storage and found another cot somewhere, and that was it. We had four adolescents in one small room; breathing and arguing and fighting and farting all over each other. Except for the farting, it may sound like sweet times, but it wasn't. The nephews regularly fought among themselves, but if you said anything at all to offend one of them the other two were on you like wasps at a summer picnic. They were quick to pound each other, but were blood-thick and you did not mess with one without incurring the wrath of the other two.

They used my mother like leeches use blood. They verbally abused her and neglected the few rules she tried to put down. Icie felt sorry for them and gave them money they didn't deserve, money she didn't have. They did nothing to help around the house. I never saw them do a single dish or sweep a single floor. They refused to cut wood and start the morning fire in our wood-burning stove. They were worthless and they were uncontrollable, unless Leroy got into the mix and suddenly, unexpectedly, took my mother's side in a matter of discipline.

And I sat in the middle of it, unable to defend my mother, unable to handle all three at once, which is what it always boiled down to—the three of them against me. I could have fought them until one or all of us bled to death and it wouldn't have made any difference. The situation was hopeless, and I grew bitter. I lost my teen years to these assholes.

During my final year of high school their dad turned up out of the blue and took over the couch in the living room. He was driving a dump truck and earning money, so I couldn't understand why he was there. He was my brother, but I didn't know him at all. I knew his kids too well by then, and now I had to contend with four of them in that tiny house. They had taken it over like settlers on the Plains.

I graduated from high school and took a summer job in a veneer plant before preparing to leave for Ashland, Oregon and my first year at Southern Oregon College. I went down to Ashland a little early to prepare for fall football practice, but also to escape the madness in my house.

The day I left I told my brother Lyle how pissed off the whole deal had made me. I told him that I thought he was a fucking bum. My brother said, "I changed your diapers when you were a baby." I said, "I don't remember that, asshole." I told him he was a piece of shit. I lit into him with five years of frustration and bitterness and I told him I'd see him dead.

That is exactly what happened. I never saw him again after I left Thompson Lane, until the day my mother buried him. I stood with her at his open casket in the funeral parlor. He had died of liver disease in Ketchikan, Alaska. He had drunk himself to death at fifty-one. The oldest of my siblings, he was the first one to pass away.

Looking down at his body in his casket, my mother cried for Lyle because she loved him. She kissed him on his ancient-looking face and poured out the tears. I sobbed for her and her alone. Watching her bury him was difficult, but I could not have cared less that he was dead.

The boys didn't come to their father's funeral. My mom talked to Leroy about it and he told her their father had made a pact with him and the other two. They wouldn't bother with funerals or sentimentality. They didn't bother with what they believed to be trifles when they lived with me, of course, and they didn't bother becoming human beings, either.

Odd Jobs

The berry and bean fields of the Willamette Valley were not my lone source of spending money every year. The harvest season lasted from June to the beginning of the next school year in early September, which left me plenty of free time to find other jobs to contribute to the scarce income my mother and I received from Social Security, benefits paid to us in the name of my deceased father. One should not wonder why my mother was an old-school Democrat and Progressive Era sympathizer. Without Social Security my mother and I would have been homeless and likely died. That is not an exaggeration.

I had a paper route when I was a kid, but not the conventional kind. I sold *Grit* door-to-door, earning ten cents per fifty-cent sale. The newspaper tabloid, subtitled "America's Greatest Family Newspaper," was published weekly in Williamsport, Pennsylvania, by the heirs of Dietrick Lamade. Dietrick Lamade had purchased the paper in 1885 and steadily grew it into a national institution. From its inception, the paper was designed to appeal to small town America. By 1932 it was available in all 48 states, and the vast majority of its circulation was in towns of less than 10,000 populations. The Lamade family famously contributed to the growth of Little League Baseball in the U.S., culminating with the erection of Howard J. Lamade Stadium in Williamsport, where the Little League World Series is held every summer. The stadium was named in honor of Dietrick Lamade's youngest son, a Little League Baseball executive.

Marketing to rural America, the paper's founder created a simple editorial philosophy: "Always keep *Grit* from being pessimistic. Avoid printing those things which distort the minds of readers or make them feel at odds with the world.

Avoid showing the wrong side of things, or making people feel discontented. Do nothing that will encourage fear, worry, or temptation…Wherever possible, suggest peace and good will toward men. Give our readers courage and strength for their daily tasks. Put happy thoughts, cheer, and contentment into their hearts."

My stack of "cheery contentment" was delivered to my house on Saturday mornings. Weekends, I would hit the neighborhood hard selling in a long and wide sweep of the area around Langmack Airport, where many middle-class families lived. By scouring the area with my papers in a heavy-canvass tote with *Grit* lettered on it in bright, bold red, I managed to build a regular clientele. I became adept at picking the right house to approach for a sale. I looked at the front lawn first. If it was green and manicured to perfection I'd approach the house and ring the doorbell. Generally, the woman of the house would answer the door and look at me like I was the cutest thing in the world, which I may have been at that time.

"*Grit*, ma'am?" I'd say. "Of course," she'd say, and I'd pull a *Grit* out of the bag, pass it to her and open my palm and take the money. At times it was ridiculously easy, but at other times I guessed wrong. I had my share of contemptuous assholes to deal with, like we all do.

I made decent cash every weekend, enough to buy a steady diet of junk food and the magazines I favored, including hunting and fishing publications, hot rod magazines, *Mad*, and an assortment of teen music magazines that I would read to learn the lyrics of popular songs, especially those by the Rolling Stones, whom I could never quite decipher without the text in front of me as I listened. Many people, especially adults, loathed the Stones, partly because Mick mumbled when he sang. I just looked the songs up to figure out what he was saying and then tried to sing along. I must say I was often surprised by what I read. Who knew?

Such is art.

I submitted my own lyrics to the magazines—they were always having "contests." Inevitably a letter would come saying I had real songwriting talent and that for a mere $50 I could have my lyrics published and presented to the stars and possibly have the songs sung on a record. My mother nixed the idea, of course, which did not bother me at all because I knew a scam when I heard one. I think I took pleasure in resubmitting one song after another, always receiving a variation of the same lame letter extolling my talent. It became something of a game I played just to see how they would express my greatness each time.

When I wasn't selling newspapers door-to-door I worked in a restaurant, Patrick's Café, owned by friends of my brother Rich. The restaurant sat on the side of Highway 20 just west of Thompson Lane. I don't recall whether laws prohibited kids from working like I did in that restaurant in the late fifties. Perhaps they did, but I managed to get around them and I became the official weekend potato peeler at Patrick's Café. Peeling potatoes was my one and only job in the café. It was the start of a sketchy career, for I would have many more potatoes to peel over the years. I stood at a double stainless steel sink on a little riser and peeled a hundred pounds of potatoes—a day's worth—and dropped them into a pot of water to be cleaned and shredded and diced by someone else before they were passed to the grill and precooked, or blanched, for morning and lunch prep.

I used to laugh when some hotshot kitchen manager years later would ask me if I ever worked in a kitchen before. I always had the standard old-timer's line in waiting. Kid, I thought, I've forgotten more about kitchen work than you've ever known. I never actually said it until I got to know my fellow workers, but I always wanted to use the line in my first interview with some particularly obnoxious culinary school graduates.

More Restaurant Work

I have had many jobs other than writing, and with few exceptions I have loathed them all. The worst of the worst jobs have been in the restaurant trade. Perhaps it is because I started working in restaurants at such a ripe young age. In restaurants I have met some of the most ignoble swine that I have been unfortunate enough to run across. The jealousy and outright pettiness inherent in the restaurant business is at times ludicrous. The rampant skullduggery is morally corrupting.

Don't get me wrong. I'm all for small businesses and artisans who are struggling to stay afloat in the margins of the business world. These people often possess a love of their venture that is inspiring. But even an honest, hardworking and committed restaurateur is susceptible to vagaries of power, unguardedly allowing ownership to commandeer his decency. In many cases you have but two choices when confronted with the fiendish restaurateur. Swallow your pride and take it in the ass like a commoner, or fight back. I tended to fight back.

I once worked for a well-known jazz club owner in Portland. One time he charged me $20 out of my under-the-table wages because I accidently poked a finger in a chocolate cake as I scrounged around the club's walk-in trying to find an item. He withheld my money and used the cake anyway. No one noticed the small puncture I'd made in the side of the cake and it was devoured by his customers without complaint. The next day I did not go into work. The owner then had the audacity to call me at home and leave a message in a cheerful voice, saying "Hey, where are you? You're late!"

I knew for a fact the swine did not pay even twenty bucks for that cake.

Another time I got into a hassle with an ignorant general manager who was recently hired at a place where I'd ran the kitchen for seven years. I'm fairly certain I knew my job, but this fellow was too dumb to see things were fine and that business was good. He thought he might tinker with things, trying to make an impression on the boss. He asked me to write a new menu, which I agreed to. I wrote it and gave it to him. What happened next is an example of the pettiness which is, in my experience, usually found in the trade. The manager gave the menu draft to a friend at a local community college. The friend typed it up, had it printed at the school, and gave the manager a very low price. That was the point. The manager had set out to save the company money by doing something on the cheap. He figured he was really on the ball.

One problem—the new menu had at least twenty typos and misspellings in it. It was awful, barely decipherable, and way below commonly known restaurant standards. I mean, come on, you want the damn menu to read like the kitchen manager (me) can spell soup (not soop) just as well as make one. I asked the manager to send the menu back. He refused, explaining that he'd already paid for the printing and he could not possibly justify reprinting it at extra cost.

Our relationship went down hill from there and he fired me. In turn he was fired by the clueless owner three months later. It took the owner too long, but he finally understood he had a moron on his hands.

I later saw the ex-manager at a mutual friend's wake and told him he'd screwed up. Without admitting it he said, "I thought about that." It was a startling confession. He'd thought about it too late, of course. We had both lost our jobs. What a swine.

My First Beer

I have been a drinker most of my life, which may explain why restaurant work first caught my fancy. The business is rife with alcoholism, naturally enough. I worked many shifts hung-over, like many of my comrades in the trade. I liked drinking after a hard shift and I've known plenty of people in the business who imbibed while they worked. Drinking and restaurant work are inseparable phenomena.

I remember tasting my first beer when I was eleven on a warm summer evening in Oakland, California. I was visiting my sister Bethel and her husband and baby girl. They lived in an apartment complex filled with other young couples. It seemed that all the tenants of that building loved to cook barbecue on the weekends. And they always had beer with their steaks and potato salad.

A shy kid, I never mingled well with adults. Visiting my sister, I stayed inside the apartment and watched television as the patio parties extended into the late evening. Adult laughter filtered through the screened patio doors, becoming more pronounced, and my sister's baby daughter crawled around on the carpeted living room floor.

I was an absent-minded babysitter, only half-watching the kid. I'd get up off the sofa and pick her up and move her away from the stereo and records, the potted plants, the bookshelves. Then I'd sit down again, growing bored, watching TV. My niece was playing a repetitive game. I was quickly growing weary. My mother had shipped me down to Oakland for a visit. I didn't have a choice in the matter and now I was regretting being there.

I was curious about the beer. I looked at the refrigerator, opened it and stared at the bottles, a brand called Blitz. Being from Oregon, where the brand was bottled, my sister and brother-in-law made sure they always had a case of Blitz around for the weekends. The bottles were lined up in neat rows on the bottom shelf. I worked up my nerve. I'd open the fridge, close it, and sit down for a few minutes. Up again moving the baby, I'd open the door once more. And close it. The baby had her interests and I had mine.

I walked to the patio door and peered out. My sister and her husband were listening to one of the neighbors tell a story. They were smiling broadly, enjoying whatever he was talking about. My sister asked me if I was hungry. I said I was thirsty. She told me to get a cola out of the fridge. No, I thought, I'd rather have a beer.

I returned to the baby, pulled her off the record pile, set her on her blanket, stuck a pacifier in her mouth and sidled over to the fridge. I saw the opener on the door hanging by a magnet. My sister came inside, surprising me. I was mere seconds from grabbing a beer. I was reaching for the opener. My sister plucked her daughter up and looked at me. Did she know? I thought she must have known, that she was reading my mind, and the thought made me feel guilty and sinful. My sister took her daughter into the bedroom and put her down for the night. When she came out she gave me a funny look and asked me if I was okay. I told her I was fine and sat down. My sister went back to the patio and her friends.

Two minutes later I got up and walked over to the fridge. I opened the door and took out a cold bottle of Blitz. I took the opener off the door and opened my first beer. They were talking about me outside. My brother-in-law said I was kind of a strange one. He said I was shy. A woman out there said I was a cute boy. I opened that bottle of beer and took a swig, my first taste. On a warm night, thirsty, bored to death, risking all, I drank my first beer. I loved it. I loved its taste, its soothing passage down my gullet, the resulting buzz. I drank that bottle dry and drank another one, sitting on the sofa, hoping my sister wouldn't come in again. But I felt rebellious, enough to think, so what? My sister might yell at me, but that would be about it. What could she do, spank me? I was already bigger than she was.

I went to bed slightly intoxicated that night. I've gone to bed buzzed many times over the years, and outright trashed on many others. I worked for many years in the restaurant trade.

I'd started early and I could drink with the best restaurant workers in the business.

Once, years ago, I saw Pete Hamill's memoir, *A Drinking Life*, in a bookstore. I snatched up a copy. Somehow I knew he had great stories to tell. Drinkers always do, particularly the dry ones.

Dreams of Journalism

I set out to become a journalist. In high school, I joined the monthly newspaper staff my senior year and became its sports editor. Winning the position wasn't based on merit, but rather on my ambition to become a sports writer after college. I don't recall anyone else even wanting the job at the time, so I thought the stars had aligned and everything would come easily.

Like most boys of my generation, I was hooked on *Sports Illustrated* from a very young age. It was one of two magazines my mother subscribed to from the time I learned to read. The other was *Reader's Digest.*

Sports Illustrated overloaded my imagination. I was awed by its stories of the great athletes' exploits, the tape-measure home runs and long, twisting touchdown runs. The magazine provided the inside information about my heroes' home towns, little glimpses of their lives, which made me envious and determined to become just like them. When that didn't work out, I thought writing stories like the ones I read in *Sports Illustrated* would be the next best thing.

I also loved the photography in *Sports Illustrated*. The pictures placed me inside the sports world in ways that sparked irresistible fantasies. In my mind, I could be sitting in Boston Garden with its odd-looking parquet floor watching a duel between two of my heroes. A close-up photo of Bill Russell and Wilt Chamberlain fighting for a rebound, elbows bent out like weapons, their heads seemingly about to touch the basket's rim—these types of images delighted me. I could spend hours thumbing through the magazine, analyzing the photos, reading and rereading the stories. And every Monday a new one arrived in the mailbox that stood on a pole at the head of Thompson Lane, where a route-driver pulled up in a car and gave me happiness.

Working on the school paper, I reported on the games my teammates and I played in the Valley Conference, a league with schools two or three times larger than mine. I learned to write slanted stories, informing readers that though we may have lost our game with South Salem Friday night, someone played heroically for the home town team. I had the power of the pen. I could make anyone look good, though I never wrote about my own performance. I understood that would be a violation of journalism's ethics. I think I actually believed that to be true, until George Plimpton brought out his bestselling *Paper Lion* in 1966, wherein *he* was the story. He and Detroit Lions defensive tackle Alex Karras made a formidable comedy team in the very least, and I learned that sports had a humorous side. They were not merely about statistics and greatness. They could be about failure as well. That's always a good lesson to grasp, because coping with failure is a skill everybody needs at one time or another in life. Plimpton said, hell, if I can't quarterback at least I can write about my inability to quarterback, which was a stroke of genius.

My year as sports editor of my high school paper inspired me to seek new heights. My teacher sent one of my columns off to the University of Oregon Journalism School to be critiqued. I'd written an opinion piece about our recent gym remodeling. The basketball court was now filled with too many lines because girls' volleyball had been added to Oregon's scholastic sports programs. Well, that was hogwash, I wrote. Nobody cared about volleyball. The floor was so overly marked now that during games our basketball team would doubtlessly be confused by all the geometry on the floor. That might cost the team a win or two over the season (I didn't mention that we had limited talent to begin with). In retrospect, the sexism of my argument was of course more the point than the argument I thought I was making. But the Oregon journalism professor liked the piece.

Then the editor of my home town weekly dropped by a basketball game one night as I warmed up on the floor, running layup drills with the rest of the team. I stepped out of the drill and he pulled me aside under one basket and offered me two-cents a word to write sports copy for his paper, the *New Era*. His name was Bill Wickland, a young, funny guy whose column was called *The Wacky World of Bill Wickland*. I loved that title, and he wrote a good column that made fun of influential people in the community and sort of rambled in every direction at once. It was a very accomplished column by a guy who had been around the world with the Navy and had much to offer homebound hick readers like me.

Bill didn't last long as editor of the *New Era*. Eight years later, when I moved to Portland permanently, Bill was working here on a monthly and recommended me for a freelance job at the paper. I got to know Bill a lot better than I'd known him when I was a young stringer. I then understood why he hadn't lasted long at the *New Era.* Having an urbane wit, an attraction to the spoils of city life, as well as a fear of physical labor, Bill was definitely not a small town kind of guy.

When I went to Southern Oregon College in Ashland, in 1969, I studied news and editorial writing and worked on the college newspaper. I wrote a baseball story with this lead:

"The average age of the New York Mets is 23 years. They are the 1969 World Series Champions. The average age of the Southern Oregon Red Raiders is 21 years. They won't be the champions of anything in the near future."

I thought it was a pretty good opening and my professor liked it, but the team—not so much.

With these early small successes I believed I had found my calling. I thought I was headed for a career in journalism. I transferred from Ashland to a community college in Albany to save money and earn an associate's degree before enrolling in Oregon's journalism school in 1971. Someone there liked my work, I knew from experience, so I figured it would be a snap. But a funny thing happened on my way to a Pulitzer Prize.

Once at Oregon, during the first quarter, the Dean of the School of Journalism called me into his office one afternoon and told me point blank I wasn't skilled enough as a writer for Oregon's tough curriculum. He said I should think about another major.

I knew he was right. Writing wasn't coming to me as easily as I thought it would, particularly the specific sort of writing the newspapers favored then and still do, which is always very tight and economical and stresses the reverse pyramid style (who, what, when, where, why and how, in order of descending importance) and has a whole laundry list of rules for punctuation and abbreviations and is very careful in quoting sources and revealing sources and...you get the picture. I couldn't do it. I had far too much to learn about writing in general, never mind the one-voice-fits-all style of the *Associated Press*. I didn't have the "ism" in journalism. I would go on writing, I realized, but just not for *Sports Illustrated* or *The New York Times*.

Now that journalism as I knew it as a young man has largely ceased to exist, it sounds silly to rue what might have been. Many former journalists my age are doing something other with their lives than journalism. In the grand scheme of things it makes no difference that I failed at journalism school. Many people agree with me that journalism itself is failing the public. The Fourth Estate is in deep trouble.

In hindsight I would venture that I had too much respect for journalism as a young man. I overestimated its value. Ultimately, news work wasn't for me for a lot of reasons, beyond the fact I couldn't master clone writing and the AP style. For me journalism really was a dream, and that dream was unlike anything actual journalists dream about. You can be assured of that. There isn't a journalist out there that can write the story you have in front of you. This story is uniquely mine, and that is good enough.

A Marvelous Paranoia

As I have said, Portland fascinated me from an early age. My oldest sister, Evelyn, lived here when I was a kid, after she divorced the millionaire rancher she lived with for a short time in Pendleton in north-central Oregon, home of the famous Pendleton Roundup Rodeo. I think Ken Kesey wrote a book about that rodeo. Maybe I'll get around to reading it someday, just not tomorrow.

My sister moved to Portland after her divorce and took a cooking job at a restaurant on 21st Avenue, in the heart of Northwest Portland, then the city's most populated neighborhood. The place was called the Dinner Bell. The old building houses another bar/restaurant now called Joe's Cellar, which is popular with hipsters and longshoremen. The longshoremen were there first, starting years ago. I can remember sitting in front of the place in a car by myself as the adults who were supposedly my overseers went inside and didn't come out for awhile. That made we wonder what the attraction in there might have been. I would discover its boozy, friendly appeal many years later.

I liked the feel of Northwest Portland from the start. I was young, but I had some fairly romantic notions about the excitement that might transpire in highly populated places. When I saw Northwest Portland for the first time I thought it must be like a New York neighborhood, full of beautiful, rustic apartment buildings and mysterious neighborhood dives, with more people on the street at any single moment than I might see on the street in my home town in a long week.

Evelyn lived in the Barker, a large four story apartment building a short walk from her job. She had a single bedroom and a roll-out sofa and I would visit, usually at the end of summer when my mother hooked a ride with a friend or other family member and we came up from mid-valley to shop for my school clothing at Montgomery Ward. My mother would charge a few things on her Ward credit card, the only card she had, and I'd have clothing for the year. Not much, but a couple of pairs of pants and a few shirts, underwear and socks and maybe a jacket if my old one had worn out or I'd grown out of it. She'd buy just enough clothing to rotate through the week and make it appear that I wasn't wearing the same clothes day after day. On weekends she'd wash the clothing in her old barrel-shaped General Electric washing machine with its dual rolling-pin rinse-compressor, which I swear performed its function better than the spin cycle in today's washing machines. Then, depending on the weather, she'd dry the laundry on four wash lines in the backyard, or hang it indoors on a folding rack that she placed near the wood-burning stove in our living room. I always had relatively clean clothes for school. Though we were poor, my mother didn't think I had to look like a *dirty mongrel* (one of her favorite expressions) as I headed out the door every morning.

The Barker, which still graces 21st Avenue, sits across the street from an old theater, one of Oregon's longest-standing movie venues—Cinema 21. It's a retro art film house now and has been for years, showing obscure movies of lesser known directors, international independent films, old classics, and the work of local filmmakers trying to break in. It's a classic old theater with a balcony, and its popcorn is still cheaper than the popcorn you'll find in contemporary multiplexes.

Sometimes Evelyn's boy Dennis and I would take a bat and tennis ball over to the schoolyard on Couch Street and play a game that was a variation of stickball. You could play many different ways, but what we did was pitch the tennis ball against the school's brick wall adjacent to the parking lot. We batted the ball off the rebound, taking turns pitching and hitting. That way, in close quarters, we hit the ball in the direction of the wall without hitting it so far that we had to chase it out into the street or retrieve it from someone's flower bed a block away. You could judge by the ball's contact with the wall whether it would have been a hit in an actual game, and that is how we advanced imaginary runners and scored the game. Hitting the top of the wall without sending the ball over the building was a home run. Anything hit over the building was an out because we had to chase the ball down, and who wanted to do that every other minute? We learned to strike the ball on a level plane, hitting line drives into the gaps of the imaginary diamond. With all my practice, one might wonder why I couldn't hit worth a damn in real baseball. But that was sure true. I turned into a good fielder, but never became much of a hitter. I guess I developed some poor swing habits in the process, not having a coach around to straighten things out, and once I did receive coaching I likely already had bad habits that were difficult to overcome.

The days in Portland were always well-spent—the round trip from the mid-valley to the city—and always produced a sense of excitement for me. For years after that I couldn't get Northwest Portland out of my system.

I moved to Portland the first time in 1973. It was summer and I lived in a rambling and extremely weathered house on Northwest Kearney. My nephew Dennis rented a room there from one of his friends and I signed on for fifty bucks a month, phenomenally low rent even then. It was the summer of the Watergate inquiry in Congress, when Senator Sam Irvin led the proceeding, attempting to get out the truth about Nixon's White House "plumbers." The hearings were incredibly entertaining television, a shocking revelation of how American politics had drifted away from people's honest concerns.

I don't think that boat has found its way back home yet, either, but the majority of Americans don't seem to be concerned with criminality in high places. Perhaps they are too inured to it, as it is now as commonplace as snow in D.C. winters. Americans are too absorbed with themselves to worry about the oligarchy that runs things now, and frankly that makes many of us appear intractably ignorant to the outside world.

My first summer in Portland I worked in a display manufacturing shop on 21st Avenue, not far from my Kearney Street room. I sanded boards all day, made them nice and smooth for the builder-craftsmen. Most display environments are now pre-fabricated or high-tech, but in those days they were built by hand out of wood. It was a thriving little business and the company would hire anybody willing to do the admittedly boring work.

I hacked it out for a summer, and enjoyed playing mushball—softball sans gloves and with a larger ball—in a neighborhood league after work. We'd hit the dive taverns that sponsored the league after the games and drink a considerable quantity of refreshments. I was always interested in dives, so when I turned twenty-one I hit them hard. There was nothing quite as appealing as legging out a homerun in mushball, working up a good sweat, and hitting the bars after the game to gloat.

That same summer, I enrolled in a poetry writing class at Portland State taught by Henry Carlile, a poet of Cuban descent who ended up teaching at the university for many years and who had learned his poetry craft at the University of Washington, with Theodore Roethke and Elizabeth Bishop. I found Henry's style to be a little precious—in the way academic poets are sometimes—though he was a fine poet. Soft and delicate, warm-hearted, searching and overly inquisitive about poetry, he strained to hear something worthwhile in everything that passed over his desk. I was an unaccomplished poet then, and I may yet be, so I appreciated his effort in looking at my poems. I heard much in that class that wasn't particularly worthy of praise, including poems of mine, but Henry would always find something to help. That was his genius as a teacher. About one of my poems he once said aloud in class, "There is a marvelous paranoia in this poem." Really? A marvelous paranoia…Was that good or bad? Or both?

I will say this regarding poetry and loosely paraphrase Carlile's mentor Roethke, who once said: everyone is a poet at twenty; some people are poets at thirty and forty. But if you're still writing poetry at fifty chances are you're a poet.

Politics and Fear

Danny Neilson, a seventh-grader, walked with a stooped carriage to begin with but that day, November 22, 1963, he walked into my sixth-grade classroom with his shoulders hunched like an old man carrying a grain sack. He paused inside the door before continuing to the center-front of the room. Standing in front of the blackboard, he announced that JFK was dead. Shot in Dallas.

The classroom fell quiet as my science teacher, Jim Riggs, suddenly stood up. He looked dazed, said nothing, and swiftly walked out of the room, disappearing in the direction of the school's offices. Danny Neilson slowly shuffled after him. The rest of us looked at each other. We were stunned. A girl began to sob, and then another. I felt a nauseous sensation crawling in my gut and a gnawing fear envelope me.

The initial memories of that day are vivid. The school buses quickly appeared outside Foster Elementary School and everybody went home early. I walked down muddy, potholed Thompson Lane from the bus stop on Highway 20. My mother and I were the only ones living at home then and my mom was watching Walter Cronkite on our flickering black and white television in the living room. The feed went to Dallas as Cronkite struggled with his voice and palpable sadness.

My memory gets sketchy after that. The next day the newspapers carried a picture of Lyndon Johnson taking the presidential oath on an airplane that sat on the tarmac at a Dallas airport. Jackie Kennedy stood beside him, wearing the same clothes she had worn in the motorcade when her husband bled on her. The jacket was pink, as the 8 mm Zapruder film and other photos would later reveal, but the picture I saw was black and white. Agony stretched across her face. Johnson looked grim and extremely tired.

Two days later Lee Harvey Oswald was being led down a basement corridor by men wearing Stetsons. Others were marching behind and to the side when Jack Ruby walked into the frame with his back to the camera. His coat fluttered open and he put a gun to Oswald's belly and squeezed the trigger. Oswald's mouth made a shape like the O in his name and he leaned over. The men around Oswald tried to cover him, but it was too late. Watching this unfold on live television, I grew frightened.

Within a week, Jackie had summoned family friend Theodore H. White to a meeting to plot the legacy of John F. Kennedy's presidency. White had won a Pulitzer Prize in nonfiction for his 1962 book about the 1960 presidential campaign, in which Kennedy fought off his rival Democrats in the primaries before beating the deplorable Richard Nixon in the general election. *I can't stand that man*, my mother often said of men who disappointed her in one way or another. She couldn't stand Richard Nixon.

The Making of the President, 1960, had created quite a stir when it came out. It was a new kind of book, a ground-breaking look at the inside of the rough edges of the campaign, written in a unique style that had more in common with novelization than old-fashion reportage. It was too new for some critics, who called it slanted, a hatchet job on Nixon, on everybody except Jack Kennedy.

Well, White was a Harvard man like Kennedy, a classmate. What the hell did they expect? With the young president murdered, White agreed to Jackie's urging to establish a suitable legacy. The subsequent myth of Camelot often looked like a kind of joke to many in the Washington crowd that revered the cutthroat business of politics. But in the lay mind, in the heartland, in a nation seeking solace, the poetry and lyre-playing that accompanied the football games on the White House lawn won out. On a boat off Hyannisport, the shimmering beauty of the Kennedy family took a firm hold on the American mind.

Teddy White had helped create the myth and, according to some, he regretted doing so. People had warned him that the Kennedy public relations machine was going too far, but out of his respect and love for Jackie he hadn't listened. The prize-winning book, which I read when the 1964 campaign was heating up, was the first book of four covering successive presidential campaigns. His second book introduced Barry Goldwater, and my mother once again said, *I can't stand that man.*

By winning the Pulitzer, White had created his own franchise with the campaign books, and they eventually lost their luster. White's luster faded as well. I had thoroughly enjoyed the first in the series, but then I lost interest in White's brand. I didn't know that before all this happened, White worked as a *Time* correspondent in China. Henry Luce, who was born in China and supported the Nationalists there, had promoted him when the young Harvard student, who specialized in things Chinese, wrote something Luce read and liked. I wasn't aware of the book White wrote in 1947 (with Annalee Jacoby) documenting the Japanese occupation of China, the American response, and the rise of Chiang Kai-shek and the coming revolution.

Thunder Out of China, when I finally got around to reading it years later, gave me many of my first insights into to how geopolitics dominate the world stage. How power and persuasion become central to peoples' national identities, and how ordinary citizens around the world are impacted by the decisions of their leaders.

Kennedy's assassination and the subsequent years of upheaval in the polity of our nation led me in a new direction, one where I began to sense there was more to life than I had imagined. I sensed that wherever it might be headed, my life would somehow be connected to politics. I began to see why Icie might say something like *I can't stand that man* with her fullest conviction, and why the statement resonates with me after many years. My thinking was becoming increasingly political and radicalized. While remaining puzzled by many of the questions confronting my life, I had at least found an opening to newer forms of inquiry through political science.

Kennedy was thrust into my life via his assassination. It took some digging to find his old friend, Teddy White, and discover a deeper meaning of the events that dominated the headlines in the 1960s—my formative years.

My Constitutional

Engaged with political ideas since my 1969 introduction
to dissent, I was moving inexorably toward what I believed at
the time might become my life's work. I'd come to Portland
in the summer of 1973 and lived in the old house on Kearney
Street that I've already mentioned, and I worked as a laborer
in a display factory. I studied with Henry Carlile at Portland
State and played mushball in a neighborhood tavern league.
And every morning throughout the Watergate Hearings I was
up early to watch the action on television.

But Portland at this time was only a wayside stop. After all, I was still a student at the University of Oregon, in Eugene. Unfortunately, I was a few credits short of graduating and I had applied for the Peace Corps, and was seriously considering leaving Eugene permanently and not bothering to finish my degree. It seemed pointless to even be there at times. By then I'd figured out that you only get from college what you put into it, and I wasn't sure I had anything left to offer. I'd taken a class on the U.S. Constitution from my favorite professor, James Klonoski, a brilliant lecturer and wit whose classes always delivered the goods, and he'd asked the class—how many of you are going to law school? I looked around and realized I was one of just a few to indicate I wasn't set on a career in law. I had never even thought about it, to be frank. The scenario jolted me. I wasn't thinking at all about law, but there I sat in a lecture auditorium with a mob of wannabe attorneys. It was bizarre. I guess I believed you couldn't be a decent American revolutionary without scorning our system of laws. Overthrowing the laws seemed to me to be the point of revolution. Wouldn't becoming an attorney be tantamount to joining the bad guys? The idea of becoming a radical attorney like William Kunztler hadn't occurred to me. And the idea of becoming a corporate attorney was ghastly to say the least.

I had taken most of Klonoski's undergraduate classes and I admired the man greatly, which is probably the major reason I was in his U.S. Constitution class to begin with. The professor fascinated and entertained me. (Is that why I was in college? Was I there to be entertained and nothing more?)

Somehow going to college and meeting career goals seemed alien to me. I had no career goals outside of some vague notion of becoming a writer, and I've explained that by this time I'd already taken a hit in journalism school—that is I lasted there about four weeks. I must have gone into a kind of shock after that. For some reason I didn't choose another path. I didn't have a plan B to fall back on, which I later discovered is the correct way to do these things. So, rather than buckling down with another discipline with obvious value I started studying politics in earnest. I liked it enormously, too, but I had no interest in law or political service; I simply found political science interesting, a kind of hobby. My degree would essentially be meaningless. It felt to me like nothing more than what any average citizen might glean from opening a copy of *Smithsonian Magazine* and booking a tour of the sights in Washington, D.C.

So there I sat in Portland at the end of the summer of 1973, waiting on the Peace Corps. When that fell through, for reasons I shall explain in the following pages, I returned to Eugene after all and took a few courses; enough to finally graduate. After graduation I was off to New England and a job not with the Peace Corps, but with its domestic equivalent, VISTA (Volunteers in Service to America). For what it was worth, I knew a little about the U.S. Constitution and the three branches of the U.S. government, but not much else. I would work in Maine for two years; my contribution to the revolution from within you might call it. I knew from the outset that my effectiveness would be limited. But I had a positive attitude and held the belief that something would fundamentally alter American society one day. I still have that belief; I'm just afraid whatever it is will come from some dark and nasty place and that many innocents will be hurt while the guilty skate once more.

Lost in New England

In 1973, as I worked slowly towards a liberal arts degree at Oregon, I believed I needed to do something meaningful with my life, so I had written to the Peace Corps. At the time I may have had some ambition to change the world—but more likely, I simply was looking for new experiences.

The Peace Corps accepted my application and I received a letter telling me I was going to Brazil, by way of El Salvador, where I would learn Portuguese.

While I grew excited about this turn in my life, the dream was short-lived. Latin American politics are famously volatile, and that was no less true in the Cold War years of the 1970s. The date of my appointment unfortunately coincided with a student uprising and street protests in Sao Paulo during a typically shaky economic time. Students were demanding jobs and lower tuition, and workers wanted more money. Doubtlessly, there were complexities exacerbating the political situation there that I knew nothing about, but the result was that the Peace Corps changed its mind and my coveted position vanished.

A part of me wondered, fantastically or not, whether I was being looked at as potential spy material. Had the government realized I wouldn't fit their profile, and so decided to leave me out of the picture? Did they understand I wasn't a fit for the pattern of coercive destabilization that was U.S. policy in South America at the time? Perhaps they received late word that I was evolving into a leftist sympathizer, and thus becoming a poor risk for the kind of covert work they had planned for me. I had protested the Vietnam War, after all, and you never knew who might be watching you under those circumstances, yes?

A few months later, I received another letter from the government offering me a VISTA position in New England. VISTA was the decade-old anti-poverty service organization started in 1964 by Lyndon Johnson. A part of his vision for "A Great Society," the agency fell under the umbrella of the Peace Corps, the Kennedy initiative to eradicate poverty in Third World nations. I still had the adventure bug and I'd never been to New England, so I immediately accepted the offer. I was living in Portland at the time, working in a restaurant near Portland State when I heard the news. Maybe I didn't have a burning desire to organize anything, but the position sure sounded better than my job bussing tables in that busy restaurant.

Within a week I boarded a Greyhound bus and rode to Seattle. I had a United Airlines ticket for a direct Seattle to Boston flight and a few things in my brother's old Marine Corps duffel bag. Soon I was on my way to Concord, New Hampshire to meet my host organization, *United Low-Income* (ULI), which was running an organizing workshop at a Concord community center nestled in the hills above town. Along with the plane ticket, VISTA had sent me a voucher for a night's lodging in Boston and a bus ticket from Boston to New Hampshire. I felt like I was being treated like an important cog in someone's wheel, which was interesting because, like I say, I really had no idea what I was in for or what this organizing gig would actually be about.

I took a cab from Logan Airport to a hotel in downtown Boston, paid for out of my own pocket. It was quite late by the time I checked in and I was tired, so I soon went to sleep, but not until I had fretted about what in the hell I was getting myself into. I was, as they say, clueless. The next morning I took another cab, this time to the Boston bus terminal and caught a local carrier bound for New Hampshire. It was October, and I marveled at the postcard scenery and vivid colors of New England's autumn. The bus stopped briefly in Lowell, Massachusetts, Jack Kerouac's hometown. (Since reading *On the Road* years earlier, I'd become a big fan.) I looked around, imagining his alter ego, Jackie Dulouz, hanging out there before becoming a football star and heading off to Columbia College, before his long journey of self-defining travels and booze binges ruined his health and killed him at forty-seven.

Outside, New England's crisp air hinted winter. I sat back in the bus and enjoyed the rest of the ride to Concord. From the Concord bus station, I jumped into another cab and the driver took me up to the hilltop community center, which I remember as being associated with a church. I also remember it being a clean, manicured place dotted with white-washed lodges and conference rooms. I found the ULI lodge, and was introduced to many people who had come from organizations all over Maine to attend this particular conference. The first evening, after various meetings broke up, some folks invited me to go with them to a bar in downtown Concord. They were all members of the Augusta office of ULI. Augusta would be my first home in Maine, but I only discovered it that night.

My hosts were ULI's director, Frank Schiller, and a VISTA liaison assigned to the organization, Bill Flynn, a Michigan grad. I had no understanding of how VISTA and ULI functioned or communicated, so while drinking and talking to Frank and Bill and others I absorbed all the details of the organization I could. We drank into the evening while I listened and learned.

I learned that ULI was a welfare-rights group. Its primary mission was to lobby the Maine legislature and the federal government to increase welfare benefits for poor families through the Aid to Families with Dependent Children program (AFDC). The organization had a lawyer/lobbyist from a state sanctioned legal group—Pine Tree Legal—and a team of paralegal advisers which assisted him, including a woman I would eventually become entangled with romantically.

Frank was a registered lobbyist, and his salary came out of funds gathered through private grants and donations by well-heeled, socially progressive philanthropies. Being a co-founder of the non-profit, Frank was an independent organizer, not a VISTA staff worker like me or the other ULI organizers with whom I drank that first night.

Organizationally, the VISTA staff was contracted to ULI through federal grants. Because we were actually employees of the federal government, VISTA staff was restricted from lobbying for a cause that might be contrary to interests who sometimes were more intent on dismantling, not expanding, social welfare. That explains why Bill, the VISTA liaison, was there. The political function of the non-profit was a delicate subject, and the feds were very sensitive about organizations threatening the primacy of their relationship to poor people.

Not much has changed politically and socially in the U.S. in the ensuing years, of course. Tension between the bureaucratic and activist organizations determined to assist the poor and those entrenched influences of the political ruling class doesn't wane based on which political party is in power.

Then why was I there? As VISTA organizers, the ULI staff in Augusta assisted people having difficulties obtaining local government assistance for services, like heating and rent vouchers. Maine towns were obliged by state law to keep a set of regulations describing eligibility requirements for localized welfare services, and since regulations varied from municipality to municipality, some were better than others. Some were virtually non-existent. And others were simply ignored by cash strapped townships whose mayors, city managers, or aldermen might be corrupt and stingy, or benevolent. In my view, all wanted the poor folks who came to the city for assistance to simply go away.

Organizing was a learn-by-doing proposition. Advocacy became the norm, and that meant doing whatever it took to secure a barrel of heating oil for a single-parent household, or getting a family's rent paid before its landlord threw the family into the street. These were chores that could be tough and at times impossible.

But, as I say, this was stuff I knew nothing about that first evening as I drank with a group of people I would come to know intimately over the following months. For example, I didn't know at the time that the various groups in the ULI coalition were often guided by jealousies and locked in petty squabbles with one another. Lewiston, the home of a tenants' rights group, had problems with the Augusta faction. Bangor's group didn't like things about Lewiston. Saco had a bitch about Biddeford. On and on. The entire experience was as much about organizational dynamics as it was about remedying social ailments. It was as much about the politics of individuals as it was about the politics of the organization. And it was *all* about the institutionalization of poverty.

So went the first night, in a blur of information and drinking. After closing the bar down, my new friends and I returned to the hilltop compound to go to bed. I'd been assigned a single room with a narrow bed in one of the lodges; I was pleased because I knew some of the others were sharing rooms. I got undressed and climbed into bed. Drunk, I soon fell to sleep. Sometime later—I have no idea when—I was awakened when someone crawled into the sack with me. She was soft and rather large. I really had no idea who she was at first. But as my beery vision adjusted to the room's half-light, I recognized her as one of the women from the Bangor Tenants' Union whom I'd met earlier in the day. Members of her group had gone elsewhere to drink evidently, because I hadn't seen her in the bar downtown.

Appropriately, we had drunken, debauched sex. Her name was Lilly, and she left my bed before first light. I don't believe I had anything more to do with her that weekend in Concord. Later, when I lived in Augusta, she visited several times and we pursued more sexual games just for their pure physicality before breaking it off. A casual encounter is all it amounted to, and that was fine with both of us.

The organizing conference took up the rest of the weekend as I adjusted to my new environment. Sunday evening everybody packed up and headed home to their various destinations in Maine. I rode with Frank and his wife in their Volkswagen bus. I can't remember what we discussed as we traveled to Augusta. Like today, I was pretty quiet, somewhat shy even, so it is possible I rode the entire trip without speaking at all.

Frank chose to show me the ULI office when we arrived in Augusta, Maine's capital. I helped him unload a few boxes of propaganda materials he'd taken to Concord; literature about the organization and the legislation he was working on with Pine Tree Legal, and a stack of the ULI newspapers called *Hard Times*. Frank said I could either ride with him and his wife to their home in Auburn outside Augusta or crash in the office if I wanted to. Either way I'd be sleeping on a sofa. I looked around the ULI office, impressed with what I saw. It had the feel of a place where big ideas were regularly hatched, while having a funky, radical décor, like something I imagined might have been in Berkeley in the 1960s.

ULI was a non-profit, and had the look and feel of one. Nothing fancy, a little tattered, clean but for a fine patina of dust that lent the space character. It looked worked-in. I liked it a lot and immediately felt comfortable and at home. I'd stumbled into something, a place and a job that filled me with anticipation.

I brought my bag up from the car and said goodnight to Frank and his wife. Frank said he'd be in early the next morning and they left. And then I was alone in the office of an organization that 48 hours earlier I didn't even know existed. I looked out the front windows and down to the street. It was after midnight and street lamps cast a soft, yellowish glow on the setting. In the days ahead I would discover a nice little café across the street and a good bar several blocks away. But for the moment I was alone, cocooned in a strange town that was only strange because I'd never been there before. But thanks to the kind efforts of the people I'd teamed up with, I felt a sense of purpose; that anything was possible, and, perhaps, good things lay ahead.

ULI was guided in its principles by the legacy of the community organizing guru Saul Alinsky. No less a right-wing luminary than William F. Buckley admired Alinsky's tenacity, calling him an "organizational genius." Buckley is sometimes referred to as the most sensible right-winger of his era, but naturally he often made me ill (sort of like George Will does today or the pseudo-intellectual columnist David Brooks, who hasn't the honesty of your average bank robber). Still, I had to agree with Buckley on Alinsky.

Hillary Clinton may have wanted to anoint Alinsky's feet in her youth, so taken was she by his vision of a truly democratic America. And Barack Obama, of course, carried the man's organizing principles to the mountain top.

No Marxist, Alinsky sought "change" from the inside. He was neither a communist nor a socialist, he said, because he wasn't a joiner. A funnier Marx, Groucho, said the same thing: "I wouldn't belong to any organization that would have me as a member." Or something to that affect.

I read Alinsky's seminal organizing bible *Rules for Radicals* in college. I loved it then and took it to heart. Required reading for community organizers, I read it hard until my eyes bled. I wore out the pages and passed it around to anyone who would listen to me. Its wisdom worked wonders for me. I was once called a "Bolshevik" by an alderman in rural Maine because I argued with him over his decision to not buy emergency heating oil for a poor woman and her brood of children. I cursed the guy, so much so that my co-organizer on the project told me I was out of line and being ridiculous. Hearing about the incident later, my project manager told me to be careful not to piss off people. You must learn the art of cajoling and kissing ass, she said. I'll try, I told her, practicing a little of the cajoling and ass-kissing she considered so important. The important fact is the lady and her children got the heating oil.

Since my time as an organizer was filled with many similar battles, I'm left to believe that Hillary, Obama and I have a lot in common. With the exception of that law degree. And the money and ass-kissing ability, of course.

Meeting Michael Harrington

I met Harlan Baker after my transfer from Augusta and ULI to a coalition partner, *We Who Care*, in Portland, Maine (my cynical friend Bob Thomas laughed himself silly upon hearing the name). The organization handled an array of community problems, from housing to welfare-rights questions, and lobbied the rich and powerful on behalf of social programs and awareness. Its offices were located in a storefront next door to a barber college, just off Congress Street, Portland's main street.

Harlan was a friendly, smiling labor organizer who dropped by frequently to discuss the topic of the day—usually politics, as Jimmy Carter had recently opened his campaign for the presidency. One day he came in and noticed my copy of Michael Harrington's *The Other America: Poverty in the United States* amid my pile of reading materials. Like Alinsky's *Rules for Radicals*, the book had biblical overtones for social activists like me who needed reference and inspirational material to carry on the cause of fighting for social justice in America. "Would you like to hear him?" Harlan asked, with his engaging smile and an innate mischievousness that I liked so much.

Harrington was scheduled to speak later in the week at the Saco-Biddeford campus of the University of Maine, a short drive from downtown Portland. As it happened, Harlan was host and designated driver for the engagement, as well as being a good friend of the renowned socialist author.

I went with Harlan as he picked Harrington up at the Portland Hilton. The experience spun my head. I was in the company of one of the greatest social thinkers who ever lived, the intellectual heir of Eugene Debs and Norman Thomas. The man who enjoyed open access to JFK and had famously influenced the former president's thinking. Here was a man who had marched with Martin Luther King. Here was a man who had committed his life, against all odds, to the cause of democratic socialism! Harrington got in and sat in the front seat as Harlan drove over to the college. I sat in back next to Harlan's pretty girlfriend, Christine.

Michael Harrington is one of my heroes, and meeting him remains one of my greatest life-events. Sensing my awe, he put me at ease with open, friendly questions about my Oregon roots, noting how much he liked the Pacific Northwest. He didn't have to ask me about my job. I was an organizer, like him, and he knew all about our line of work.

A founder of the *Democratic Socialist Organizing Committee*, Harrington had some time before split with America's hard-line socialists, whom he believed were drifting towards a totalitarian ideology suspiciously related to Soviet communism. For Harrington, socialism was a democratic ideal. His interests lay in reformulating the American system to create an economically inclusive democracy, ideas he elucidated in 1972's *Socialism: Past and Future*, a book I believe to be as relevant to America's present disposition as it was in 1975, the year I met the author.

At the college, the academics seized Harrington and took him to the stage where he sat as someone from the political science department introduced him.   Naturally the introduction went on too long, embarrassing Harrington, who I briefly fantasized might cut the man short by clubbing him on the head with his notebook.

Harrington got up and talked about the current role played by the Organization of Petroleum Exporting Countries (OPEC) in destabilizing the Middle East. A gasoline shortage was then gripping America. He spoke for an hour, before mingling with whoever wanted to talk to him for another hour. When it was all over, Harlan drove us a few blocks to a bar in downtown Saco, a small city about 15 miles south of Portland.

Harlan opened the door of the bar for Harrington, and as he walked in the crowd parted like a sea of fans at a championship prize fight. The bar crowd showered him with love, and it dawned on me that the place was filled with activists, graduate students and professors, all of whom had been waiting for him. A big round table in back was prepped. Pitchers of beer were already set up. Somebody offered Harrington a chair. He sat down first as the honored guest and as many as could fit around the table joined him.

We drank and talked until closing, though I mostly listened and drank. Being one of the youngest and most inexperienced people in the room, I was hesitant to raise my voice. People came and went, taking turns sitting at the table, asking questions and voicing opinions. It was civil, but as with any political discussion elements of difference crept into the proceedings. The beer made some too brave. Harrington was wrong about this or that. No, he was right on. People compromised and laughed. Tempers flared briefly and were extinguished just as fast.

We drove Harrington back to the Hilton and said good night. I told him what a great pleasure meeting him had been and he remained cordial, tipsy but in control, flushed from the beer and relaxed. Harlan walked him to his room and Christine and I stayed behind in the car. I turned to her. "How about *that?*" I said. "Incredible," she said. She was as impressed as I that we had spent the evening with this greatest of men.

Harlan dropped me off at my place and I rolled into bed, but I had trouble getting to sleep. I kept thinking about the evening, the incredible experience I'd just had, a night I haven't forgotten, nor ever will.

Later, in the summer, I joined Harlan and Christine in a NAACP march in Boston. I ran in and out of the march, snapping photos. I have some good ones of Harrington and Harlan marching together proudly under the bright red DSOC banner.

Sadly, Harrington died too young, in 1989 at sixty-one, from throat cancer. Before he died he was instrumental in coalescing American socialists in a new organization, the *Democratic Socialists of America.* Harrington loved socialism and democracy. He held great hope. Moreover, he loved people, for whom he carried his great vision of economic justice. I think about him and that night all the time. That night and the Boston march were the only times I met the man, but they were enough. To this day I believe his ideas are right.

Regulating the Poor

The study of history is in part the study of hierarchies. I have a particular fascination with the historical underdog, no doubt because I have always felt like one. The ongoing story of my life is the struggle I have with poverty. I am poor now, most writers are, except for the very few mega-talents who crack bestsellers lists, and except for those lucky others who may not have top talent but have managed to forge the right connections (including those who've connected with their readers' abysmal tastes).

Bestsellers are often crap. Publishing is marketing, in the main, and many worthy books never make it to those lists, or even get published. Who knows how many talented writers penned their opuses before dropping out and becoming shoe salesmen? Ah, such is life.

I don't resent the Jean Auels of the world, though I cannot read them. They've obviously made something work for themselves, and that is a talent in itself. Good for them.

What I do is often spoken of disparagingly as "vanity publishing." I liken the process to the early era of mimeo publishing. When I was a kid every school had mimeo machines, just like most schools now have computers. When you wrote something, you slapped it on the mimeo and churned out copies for your teachers, friends and classmates. It was cool. Your little essays, "How I Spent My Summer Vacation," or the love poems to your would-be girlfriend, were put out to the world. To this day, if you write something sweet for a girl she might kiss you. Now you can make it look better is all, darn near professional. That is the story of my *Round Bend Press*. It's my effort to be kissed rather than kissed off.

We'll see.

Returning to poverty and hierarchies—I have written elsewhere in this book about Saul Alinsky being mandatory reading for community organizers when I worked as an organizer in the early '70s. Another book, mandatory for organizers with *United Low-Income*, was Frances Fox Piven's and Richard A. Coward's *Regulating the Poor: The Functions of Public Welfare.* This was the first book I read that clarified for me the growing dissatisfaction I had developed as a young person for corporatism and its connection to welfare programs in the U.S.

Distracted by sports and much else as a youngster, I had never thought too much about my poverty. But I knew too well that I had lost my father when I was an infant, and that my mother struggled to feed, clothe and house three fatherless home-bound children. In an age before food stamps, we ate U.S. agricultural commodities passed out monthly by the county. We ate a lot of free government cheese (which, I readily admit, made great toasted cheese sandwiches). And we drank a lot of powdered milk. I had the requisite paper route and picked crops every summer next to my smart but uneducated mother, wore hand-me-downs, rued my poor dental health, and generally did without everything except the necessities. But of course even the necessities were often skimpy, too. Our plumbing never worked, so we shit in No. 10 coffee cans and buried the feces in the open field behind our house. I used to go out furtively after dark and bury shit. I also kindled the morning fire in the winter, as our heating source was an old wood-burning stove. We had to buy the wood naturally, and sometimes we ran out at the most inopportune time.

When wood-burning stoves became vogue decades later I thought it quaint. I had learned to hate wood stoves!

My early years were like a long camping trip in the wilds, burying the shit and eating rations packaged in plain white and black wrapping. But it was a fairly normal life for a poor kid like me.

Well, eventually a man learns and moves forward as best as he can. I had the benefit of college, true, which most poor kids didn't have. But college in those days didn't cost very much. Anyone could get it done if they really wanted to. I worked in a veneer plant for three summers during my college years, as the job paid well for the times. I suppose I could have kept that job, made a career of it, and probably purchased a house and a boat. Some of my family did that sort of thing. Not me, I had bigger plans. They never really panned out, but I sure had them. And I'm glad I did.

Today, education is big business. Everything is business. President Calvin Coolidge said: "The business of America is business." Given that, America is also teeming with highly educated, underemployed people, an unhealthy reality. Eventually you start thinking about how business works. You read a little Marx, you get a job that doesn't feel right, then another and another, and you soon realize the system is a set up. The rich need you, the old money need you. The career ladder is not for all. Most people stay poor and feed the beast. Only a few make it to the top. Everybody else is a functionary, force-fed television, or escaping to sporting arenas, or church. And to top it off the inevitability of Murphy's Law takes hold: The leaders, the careerists who have made it, are often blithering idiots—spoiled cream rising to the top.

113

Well, if you are poor yet managing to do what you love none of this matters. That's where I am now. It's been a long road. I've cast off every illusion I'm capable of casting off, except the one that says *Round Bend Press* has a chance and may mean something someday. It has given me tremendous satisfaction, which makes me happy, though I haven't made a dime on it at the time of this writing. I may never make a dime. I don't worry about it. There is always a minimum wage job. Well, not always, not in 2010, as this is being written. Not in this recession that looks more and more like a full-blown depression. This looks like one of the worst economic situations in U.S. history, and certainly the worst in my lifetime.

Nothing I've written in this chapter is a secret, of course. Everybody knows if they stop and think about it that the game is rigged, that poverty is a necessary evil. Anything else would be derided as *socialism*, a word that is anathema to those who continue to manipulate the poor.

I Did Not Go to Vietnam

Wars, even the necessary ones, are folly. Rudimentarily, we know why wars happen. We know they spring from inhumane impulses and ignorance. We know the corrupting nature of avarice and the geopolitical realities that propel conflict. We know that the lust for power is systemic and that unrestrained nationalism plays a role. We understand the psychology of war.

The impulse to war sits in front of us like a morsel of strychnine laced with rat poison. Yet we bite it off and swallow it. Like Vietnam, where France clung to its colony until the bitter end and was finally routed by a people seeking the ideal we supposedly fought for in Europe—actual freedom. The hypocrisy of the epoch astonished Graham Greene and seemed worthy of a novel, *The Quiet American*. Greene had seen the brutality of the French close-up in Vietnam, reporting for the London *Times* and *Le Figaro*. In creating quiet Alden Pyle, a naïve and privileged American, Greene wasn't about to let American duplicity off the hook in 1955. A decade later, America had taken over the war in France's stead, and the tragedy of America's own neo-imperialistic adventure began to play itself out.

Only fourteen at the time, I wasn't paying very close attention. My brother, however, had served in Vietnam in an "expeditionary" role as the slow buildup and evolving commitment to counterinsurgency spun out of control under Presidents Kennedy and Johnson. At that time, America was limited to an advisory role in the Nam, forbidden to exchange fire with the Viet Cong rebels or North Vietnamese regulars. Incoming mortars smashed my brother's battalion as it built landing strips near the Ben Hai River, south of the Demilitarized Zone.

Before I graduated from high school in 1969, a school counselor had suggested I nab a deferment and go to college instead of joining the Air Force, which had been my vague plan. He had asked me why I was considering the Air Force, and I had told him the truth. I saw it as an alternative to the draft and the Army infantry. I was not fully aware at the time that Air Force and Navy enlisted men were also dying in Vietnam. Though we had studied "current events" during my senior year, my teacher was a rabid anti-communist named Mr. Johnson (no relation to Lyndon), and he never bothered to probe too deeply into the details of the war. However, he did have a habit of reading letters from his former students who were in Vietnam at the time or had recently come home from the war. Noticeably missing was any letter from Harley Dimmick, a friend of my nephew Dennis, who didn't make it home. Mr. Johnson was a patriotic cheerleader who felt certain that crushing communism and blocking the "falling dominoes" in Southeast Asia was the right course for America. To please him, I wrote a paper on the evils of communism. I parroted his views and he loved the paper, giving me a rare A for the class. Like most kids I couldn't know enough about the particulars of the war to understand, much less believe, what I had written. I had merely

117

succumbed to the pro-war propaganda. My teacher had not done me a favor by accepting my weak, uninformed effort, but I doubt even he understood how he was corrupting history as it unfolded around him.

Of course I was as naïve about Vietnam as Greene's Alden Pyle. Had I been honest or less cowed by the authority of the educational system I might have simply stated the truth. I didn't know anything about Vietnam. All I really understood is fear. And I didn't want to end up dead. Nor did my mother want me to die. In fact, she had hid the truth of my brother's service from me—actually she simply lied to me. The entire time my brother was in Vietnam she told me he had a desk job in Okinawa. True to begin with, it had changed as the U.S. was drawn deeper into the war. With thousands of others he made the short flight from Okinawa to Vietnam when his time came to fight.

Perhaps my mother wanted to believe the lie herself. I later realized she did not want me to worry; she worried enough for both of us. My brother did finally ship back to Okinawa unscratched just before the Battle of Ia Drang Valley in November, 1965, when the killing in Vietnam escalated.

118

When he left the Marines a year later he didn't return to our small Oregon town, except to visit briefly before settling in the San Francisco area. By the time I visited him in Fremont, south of Oakland, in 1972, he was married and the father of a baby girl. But I could tell something was seriously wrong.

My brother and I stood in sharp political contrast. I had been radicalized in college and I hated the Vietnam War with an abiding passion. My brother hated war protesters with equal force. Thus began a long stretch of hostility between two brothers born six years apart but separated by a war and rapidly changing American culture. I looked for a long time for the root meaning of our differences. I had become politicized in the middle of a great cultural change. When he joined the Marines in 1962 there were a few hundred American advisers in Vietnam, and any number of Alden Pyles. At first what they were doing there promised to be short-term. And then it turned to disaster and tragedy for everyone concerned.

That the U.S. thought it might supplant the French and save capitalist imperialism in Southeast Asia was of course folly. Few Americans knew it at the time, but that would change

119

with the first flush of rising body counts. Six short years later, even Lyndon Johnson knew what many high school counselors in small town America knew. Vietnam was a quagmire and they were advising their students to stay clear of it. My counselor had, without tipping his hand. All he said was think about it. That was enough.

I did not get drafted and go to Vietnam or join the Air Force. I did not suffer a pang of patriotism and volunteer to save America from communism. I feared war, not communism. I did not go to Vietnam because I did not want to kill people— or be killed—for a cause I knew nothing about.

So I took my counselor's advice and nabbed a student deferment and went off to college like a good kid. It was a fortuitous time for me, a narrow escape. Sadly, my fortuitous time was a tragic time for many young men my age. I cannot help but draw parallels to today's tragedies in Iraq and Afghanistan. Young Americans are dying. I hesitate to say the cause is just, because nothing in my mind or soul tells me it is.

San Francisco Blues

Lawrence Ferlinghetti was one of the Beats, but not quite one of the Beats. I walked into his store in San Francisco one day in 1976, and he spotted me, peered at me over a low expanse of shelving. I could feel his eyes tracking me as I slowed. I paused at a table and looked at a stack of books.

I think Ferlinghetti thought I might be a thief. I wasn't, but as a businessman, he had to be sure. You don't survive in the bookstore business for nearly sixty-years without paying attention to who walks through the door. That said, it is quite likely he was merely curious about everything—even me.

I looked up from the table of books and he was still watching me. I nodded, smiled. He nodded back. He realized I was okay. He returned to shelving books and I continued to browse.

I've always liked Lawrence Ferlinghetti. Of the San Francisco Renaissance poets, including the Beats, of which he is and isn't, he has always been one of my favorites. Certain of his works still stun me by their translucent simplicity and perfectly structured imagery.

I didn't speak to Ferlinghetti that day. As I was screwing up my nerve to approach him, a few of his neighborhood friends drifted into the store and they huddled together to talk. I browsed some more and finally left. I walked across the street to Vesuvio Cafe and ordered a beer. I sat down at a window table in this sacred place and watched Columbus Avenue go by.

I was right in the middle of it all. North Beach was the heart of the greatest literary movement in my lifetime, but the movement consisted of stragglers now. I'd see Bob Kaufman on the street, a few others, but most were either hiding or gone. I was only twenty years too late to see the movement close up. Kerouac was dead, which is all I needed to know about how literary movements flash through the sky and burn out of flame.

I'd met Lyn in Waterville, Maine. She lived in San Francisco, but she was in Maine visiting her father when she called my office. Her father was an alcoholic, and she was staying with him. Neither of them had rent money. Would I help them and talk to the city manager? I met Lyn at city hall and we talked to the man in charge about a rent voucher. He relented under my persuasive assault and—presto—Lyn's father had another month to stay at home and drink.

Naturally grateful, Lyn invited me to spend Thanksgiving with her and her dad. The old man said hello and slinked into his room. He drank in his room alone, rarely coming out. While he busied himself by drinking himself to death, Lyn and I made out on the sofa.

Then, in early December, she returned to San Francisco. I'd known her a total of three weeks. From San Francisco, she wrote me long love letters. "When you are finished there, come here," she said.

When summer arrived, with Lyn on my mind, I was ready to go to San Francisco. So I left Maine and never returned. That wasn't the plan at the time; that is simply what happened. I liked Maine, but now I had something else to chase—another dream. A woman.

Arriving in San Francisco, I moved in with Lyn, her nine year-old daughter Trina, her hardware-salesman roommate, Richard, and his dog Cosa, a friendly Doberman. The Richmond neighborhood flat where they lived, a mere block from Golden Gate Park, was long and narrow with a back porch that looked out toward the ocean and a beautiful view of the city. I felt instantly at home in the roomy flat, but the feeling wouldn't last long at all.

Lyn was bartending at a place on Clement Street when I arrived. She seemed happy to see me, but already I'd noticed something different about her. The letters had dropped off weeks before. A lot of their romantic appeal had vanished. What the hell, I thought; she's just busy with work and her daughter. I would learn soon enough that she had more going on in her life than I imagined. Well, I did imagine it, but I was in denial.

Lyn took after her dad a bit, and drank heavily. She drank as she worked when her customers bought her drinks all night. She was popular, attractive, smart and adept with a line of bullshit. She had a big following at the bar; much bigger than I imagined.

She got angry with me one night when I came into the bar. "Don't come in here so much," she told me. "I'm working and you're a distraction." Later, I got into an argument with one of her regulars and stormed out of the bar before the incident escalated into violence. She closed the bar and came home very late as usual, smelling of something with licorice in it. We argued about my near fight with her regular and then she told me about Bob the mailman, a friend who was helping her out. He gave her a hundred dollars every time he helped her out. All she had to do was sleep with him.

I moved out the next day, finding a furnished room in a big boarding house in Haight-Ashbury, at Cole and Haight. The house was at the end of the park, down from Stanyan, the street the poet Rod McKuen rhapsodized over in his popular book, *Stanyan Street & Other Sorrows*. It wasn't a book I cared for, but it was a rare poetry book inasmuch as it became a bestseller. That doesn't happen often in the U.S., so perhaps I should find a copy, reread it, and figure out why it sold so damn well, but I think I may already know the irrational answer.

I was working as a sub-sandwich shop manager for a small chain operation. I'd walked in cold and asked for a job and within weeks I was a sub-sandwich shop manager on Geary Boulevard at Arquello. Running the show, I was free every day by lunch hour, assigning work to my crew and leaving to go to Candlestick to watch the Giants, or drifting through the barroom scene in the Richmond District. The neighborhood had many Irish bars in it, so I usually drank a Guinness to start off around noon every day. Then I'd switch to a lighter lager, or an Anchor Steam bottle. I had to be careful not to get too blistered before heading back to the shop around 2 p.m. to see how lunch sales went. I'd make sure everyone did their little cleanup and stocking chores, count and deposit the receipts, double check everything and then call it a day. Managing that place, I grew sort of lazy. Sometimes I wonder if I've ever recovered from the experience.

So I'd finish the day and head over to Vesuvio's, sit around there for awhile and have a little more beer right in the middle of the long-gone poetic Renaissance. It was then that I walked into the City Lights Bookstore and saw Ferlinghetti. I wasn't just any damned tourist. I had a job and lived in the Haight for God's sake!

I was living in Portland a few years later when Ferlinghetti came up to the Northwest to participate in the Portland Poetry Festival. He sat on a panel with a group of writers. William Stafford and a few others gave brief lectures on poetics, and when it was Larry's turn he got up, a tall, wiry man, and said "Light!" Then he said it again and again. "Light! Light! Light! Light!" He said it many times, his voice growing louder and louder. He began to dance with the word. "Light! Light! Light!" Then he sat down without saying anything else. That was all, a minimalist poem and a non-lecture.

Rain at the Border

My friend Bob Thomas drove down to San Francisco from Lebanon, Oregon in his cherry 1965 Chevrolet pickup and helped me move out of my place off Taraval, the main street along the oceanfront south of downtown. Taraval had a street car line, and I rode it daily to a bus stop to connect with my Geary Street bus and my job at the sandwich shop.

I'd moved from Haight-Ashbury six-months earlier, having met a woman who owned a small shop next to my workplace. She was Taiwanese and owned several properties around town. She gave me a great deal on my new place off Taraval, but I immediately regretted the move. In the Haight I could always find something to do, day or night. Several great music venues were located within a short walk from my place on Cole and Haight. Neighborhood cafes, small delis, bookstores and Ma and Pa grocery stores lined the street.

My new place on the southern edge of the Sunset neighborhood had nothing but single-family housing with an occasional apartment building thrown into the mix. Suddenly I had nothing to distract me except books and a small radio— I didn't own a television. This was coming off months of hyperactivity, listening to bands in the clubs on Haight every weekend afternoon, hitting a jazz club in the evening that took me about two minutes to walk to from my room, browsing book and music stores, and generally losing myself in the neighborhood's vibes.

At the same time the owners of the sandwich shop were rapidly expanding and were pressuring me into thinking about my "five-year plan" with the company. The term had always freaked me out, as I knew I wasn't prepared to think about long-term employment with any firm, much less a fucking sandwich shop. A steady diet of ham and turkey and meatballs (we had a great meatball recipe)? Surely there was more to life than that!

The excitement of the sub shop was underwhelming to say the least, though I did have regular customers who were members of the University of San Francisco basketball team, which was ranked number one in the country for most of the 1976 season. Bill Cartwright, who as a sturdy veteran later played for the Chicago Bulls in their Michael Jordon-led glory years, was a regular 7' 1" patron, along with 6' 9" James Hardy and others, including some of their mothers. Cartwright's mother was unbelievably nice, a smart woman with an infectious sense of humor. She was justifiably proud of her USF boys, and she wasn't afraid to admit it, either. I can even see Cartwright now, coming down the street with his shorter teammates for a few sandwiches, wearing very large shoes and a smart golfing cap. He was a big man, even in big San Francisco.

The Haight had changed for the better since the flower children era of the previous decade, but it hadn't yet turned completely to gentrification, either. (Northwest Portland once reminded me of the Haight. It too would change.)

Like many young people, I was restless, searching for ideal living conditions that were nonexistent, because the ideal is in one's head, not any particular place. I had in the course of four years moved four or five times; twice from Eugene to Portland, once to New England where I lived for two years, and then to San Francisco, where I lived for just a year and a half. Now I was headed home to Oregon. When you factor in that I went to four different colleges over a span of five years, I spent most of the 1970s on the road.

But I wasn't done looking for place quite yet. When Bob Thomas picked me up in San Francisco in early 1977, we drove back to Oregon and I stayed at his place in Lebanon, where Bob worked for his family's car dealership. I'd met Bob and his fraternal twin, John, in Ashland, in 1969. I lived in the room next door to them in Forest Hall. They were freckled redheads with outstanding comedic sensibilities and political tastes similar to mine. I liked them immediately.

On the first day we were together in Ashland, John and I were playing football on the administration building's lawn when I accidently put an elbow in his eye, knocking him out

132

of the game. I can't recall exactly how it happened, but John was quarterbacking and I was blocking for him and somehow his face and my elbow got entangled. He disappeared immediately, but I knew his dorm room was next to mine, so I knew where to find him. Later, feeling bad for the poor fellow, I knocked on his door and Bob answered; only I wasn't aware he was John's twin. I said, "Gee that was a speedy recovery, John. I thought you were really hurt." That is when Bob swung the door open fully and I could see John lying face down on his bed nursing the black eye I had given him.

Bob may have mumbled something like, "Him, not me." Bob could be sullen and always seemed to be in a deeply meditative state bordering on anger. Eventually I learned to appreciate his personality, his droll and cynical worldview, his darkness. Bob understood, whereas perhaps I didn't at the time, that humanity had a dark side that was absurd and unrelenting. He hadn't faith that mankind had much purpose beyond eating, shitting, sleeping and procreating at ill-advised times. Bob and John were inseparable in Ashland, yet they couldn't live together. Shortly after meeting them and hanging out together I moved in with John and Bob took a room alone down the hall. Peace suddenly settled on the first floor of Forest Hall on the campus of Southern Oregon College.

Bob and I loaded his pickup with my stuff and hit the road out of the Bay Area for Oregon and Lebanon, where I eventually went to work selling—or rather trying to sell— cars for John and Bob's father. When Bob and I crossed into Oregon (I-5 is mountainous at the border) we drove straight out of California sunshine and directly into an Oregon rainstorm. No kidding. We stopped under the "Welcome to Oregon" sign and fastened a rain tarp over my gear.

I was a horrible car salesman and I deservedly got canned, but later found a job in a mobile home factory and settled in for a few months during the spring and early summer of 1977. I had grown up near Lebanon and knew I didn't want to live in the area permanently, and so my thoughts naturally began to wander back to Portland, the city I had loved since childhood. But before that happened, the brothers Thomas and I had some great times in Lebanon and some very dull ones as well.

Old Ed's Briefcase

When I'd met them seven years previously, Bob and John's sibling rivalry was interesting, an affair of clashing wills and one-upmanship that settled over our college dorm like a black cloud. We lived on the first floor of Forest Hall and I think everyone there was relieved when the twins finally separated and Bob took a solo room, allowing me to ditch my roommate Phil, whom John had taken to calling "Nightmare Phil" because his countenance resembled nothing less than a spirit in the constant confusion of a bad dream.

Bob and John were political activists and had taken to the streets during the Vietnam Moratorium of 1969, a nationwide teach-in on the war. American campuses, fired by protest, surged into near anarchy and constant countercultural activity, urged on and inspired by Country Joe McDonald's *Fixin' to Die Rag*, The Doors, The Dead, Quicksilver, et al. The brothers insisted I tag along on their rebellious journey.

I would learn much besides politics from the brothers. When I moved to New England to begin my short-lived career as a community organizer, Bob mailed books to me that he picked up at another friend's store. He sent me the Pocket Poets Series from City Lights, among many others, introducing me to several poets I was unfamiliar with at the time, most notably Kenneth Patchen, whose poetic powers continue to engage me.

I hadn't been very political growing up. Paying attention infrequently, I'd read little history and hadn't grasped the nuances of struggle, or any complete historiography, or the perpetual epistemologies of inquiry and skepticism. Rather I absorbed a corruption of history as it was typically taught in high school. In my education, history was reduced to a rote exercise, which wasn't entirely the fault of the curriculum. Some educators then, as now, were simply not up to the task, lacked imagination themselves, and hardly took their employment seriously enough to open education to any potential it might have for the actual lives of students.

Without being an educator intimately involved with today's curricula it is difficult for me to see how much of this systemic function has changed. But in my daily meetings with all the "Nightmare Phils" of the world I would argue history has yet to seize the imaginations of enough people to counter the utter corruption of facts.

The Thomas brothers were great first-year friends in college. And they propelled my education forward. Though my age, they were smarter, two of the smartest people I had ever met.

So, it was seven years after we'd met that Bob helped move me to his place in Lebanon. He shortly thereafter introduced me to Ed, a salesman in his sixties. Ed worked at the Thomas family's dealership and Bob was excited that I should meet the "old man," whom he described as an adventurous character, a man whose own rebellion inspired Bob in deeply felt ways. Ed owned a fishing boat that worked out of Depoe Bay, crewed by a pair of his sons. He lived part of the year on the Salmon River at Otis, a tiny hamlet outside Lincoln City on the coast. His Silver Stream trailer sat on the embankment of the river, under the constant threat of the stream's winter crest. He was an accomplished salesman, so he quit and returned to the auto lot in a predetermined seasonal schedule that only the best salesmen are allowed to keep. With his trailer on the river and his boat and kids at sea, Ed had a busy kingdom to watch over. He seemed to always be on the move, demonstrating a kinetic energy that belied his age.

Bob told me about Ed's briefcase. Inside it the old man toted three important supplements to his lifestyle; a bag of good pot, a vial or two of cocaine, and a pistol. Because Ed was a salesman you could have imagined that contracts and note pads might have been usefully stashed in the briefcase. But Ed kept those things elsewhere. The briefcase was reserved for a well-planned, specific purpose—it held cocaine to clear his mind of the influences of normal society, pot to mellow him out and take the edge off, and a weapon in case anyone objected too harshly.

Ed was, in Bob's fluid imagination, a Hunter S. Thompson sort, without pretense or affectation. Old Ed had simply evolved into such a man without the influences of literature or a calculated turn of style. To Bob, Ed was an authentic man devoid of questions regarding the purpose of life, an able and focused rebel with a clear philosophy and reactive in the sense that simple rules provided reckoning—if anybody set out to harm him he had the answer. In fact, he held the answer to everything in his briefcase.

The beauty of the thing was the idea that if any person tried to take Ed's drugs he would simply open his suitcase, give them the drugs, and then shoot them. Knowing this, the addicts wisely stayed away. The police, had they known, wouldn't bother him. Justice would be served in a classical, counter intuitive era of some sort of beatific cultural revolt as it played in rural Oregon, pinioned by a sense of "small town" justice and rationale.

That was a long time ago, of course. You might call it history. I do. Before drug wars reached their ache of insanity, and before drug repression became normative, Bob and I occasionally indulged with Ed. And when we did, a residue of whiteness covered Bob's coffee table. In a house clouded with marijuana smoke and glutted with empty beer cans, Bob played Waylon Jennings and Jessi Colter on his stereo as Old Ed smiled at the ceiling and closed his eyes.

Flophouse

When I finally moved to Portland to stay in 1977, I rented a small room in a flophouse on Everett Street. It hadn't the amenities I had in my San Francisco boarding house at Haight and Cole, but it was the best deal I could find after searching all day for a reasonably priced place to dwell. The room was down a long corridor wallpapered with colored photos clipped from magazines, taped into position, or hung loosely with single stickpins, so they had a tendency to roll up rather than remain flat against the wall. The room was furnished with a gas cooking stove—a small bonus in a drab environment—a refrigerator, some cramped cupboard space.

A lone window offered a view of a hedge in an adjacent backyard. I would have liked a better view but couldn't argue with the monthly rent

I had come to town to try to write after spending two interesting but somewhat futile years as a political organizer in New England, and a couple more managing a sandwich shop, before brief experiments as a car salesman and factory worker. I had always wanted to lead a good literary life, but my idea of a literary life had grown mainly out of the biographies of a few dead writers whose work I admired. But I was twenty-six, with youthful ambition, and I soon started freelancing for a monthly community newspaper. The money in my savings account, wages I'd earned in the Lebanon, Oregon factory, would keep me in food and drink for a month. After that I'd have to go to work at something besides writing to make ends meet. But I was in no hurry. For some time I kept quietly to myself, seldom speaking to the other occupants of the house, mainly elderly pensioners. Every morning I heard them coughing and wheezing in the communal bathroom that adjoined my room. The sounds depressed me at first, but by afternoon I always recovered a sense of joy at not having to work, appreciating the cheap room and my tolerable elders.

I'd been working hard on a cycle of poems I've long since lost or destroyed. I wrote every morning and listened to jazz in the afternoon, usually with a bottle of wine at my side, managing to feel good about my decision to leave the repetitious factory job and move to Portland.

In the middle of my second week in the house a neighbor knocked on my door. It was a September afternoon and I was listening to jazz.

"Is that Charlie Parker?" The neighbor was a short, plump fellow with a mop of hair that reminded me of the early Beatles. "Unbelievable," he cried. "I haven't heard any decent music in weeks!" He said his name was Alex, and throughout the next weeks he would become both friend and pest. I introduced myself to Alex and offered him a coffee mug of wine, which he happily accepted, glancing around the room for a place to sit down. "My room is a little bigger than this one," he said as I cleared off a portion of my writing desk and invited Alex to sit in my uncomfortable work chair. I turned Parker down and refilled my own cup with wine, wondering whether I really wanted to socialize just then.

"Are you a writer?" Alex said, looking at the bulky old Royal typewriter I used in those days. I was disappointed in his question because writing was the last thing I wanted to discuss. To this day I dislike talking about writing, which is always a too personal matter to share with strangers. I've always felt that to discuss writing is to jinx the process. It's better to just write and hope for the best, hope the muse carries her weight and allows you to accomplish something meaningful when you sit down at the desk. "I'm giving it a go," I said, and Alex flashed a mischievous grin, understanding instantly that I wasn't going to offer much about my work. He changed the subject: "This is really something, isn't it? I think we're the only ones here under seventy."

We spent the next hour or so talking. Alex had just finished his undergraduate work at the University of Illinois and on a whim had decided to visit Oregon. He'd heard a lot of good things about Portland, so he decided to see for himself. He was impressed by the city's natural and architectural beauty and the fact that you could walk everywhere. "I'm staying," he said. "I love it here and my girlfriend Karen is coming out in two months." Karen was Alex's soul mate who he'd met at the university. She was from a small town in southern Illinois and he was from Chicago. Hating Chicago's winters, he had always wanted to move to a smaller, warmer city.

Alex was nice enough and we had a good visit, listened to a few more jazz records before it was time for him to leave. As he left he said, "Have you met Tania by the way?" I hadn't, I confessed, but I had several times seen the small, fragile woman he described. She lived two doors down from me at the end of the hall. She was always cooking, I knew, because I could smell the fragrance of what I imagined were excellent meals. I told Alex I'd introduce myself to her the next time I saw her. "You should," he said. "She's an incredible old woman."

I became set in a routine, writing, sipping wine, listening to music. And Alex became something of a fixture, dropping by all the time to chat and tell me about his latest adventures. His enthusiasm for music, literature, beer and conversation was boundless. One evening he brought Tania to my room and introduced us and the session turned into a long night of kibitzing and laughter. More sessions followed and I fell into a pattern of listening and enjoying Alex and Tania's chatter. Eventually, as I knew I would, I grew tired of it and wished I had a little more solitude in the evenings, particularly after I took a job in a nearby restaurant where I had to deal with hundreds of customers and my co-workers every day.

I found a bar on nearby West Burnside Street that I liked. It had recently been remodeled into two large comfortable rooms and it became my hideaway. It was named the Kingston Tavern and I liked the place because the booths in the low-key dining area were fitted with lamps that produced a soft, mellow light excellent for reading. Most nights I took my books there and read far into the evening, happy to leave Alex and Tania to each other and their rooms.

I worked at keeping my writing a daily routine, often writing in long hand in the Kingston. When it wasn't going well, which was frequently, I turned my attention to serious beer drinking. I got to know the staff and I would soon start to work there as a cook, a job that didn't last very long because the manager disliked me for some reason, which I never really understood, except that I may not have been quite hip enough for his taste. He thought he was God's gift, but he was really just another egoistic restaurant manager, which meant we were destined to have a personality conflict from the start. It didn't take long before Alex found me at the Kingston and my hideaway was exposed. He would slide into my booth, usually uninvited, and begin to talk his habitual million words a minute. As he slashed through various topics he kept a pen at ready, scribbled notes, drew abstractions in his notebook, and chain smoked Vantages. There were times in the ensuing days when I simply could not tolerate Alex's company and tried to avoid him. I found a couple of other joints to hang out in just to get him off my trail. Though we remained somewhat friendly, something about his personality irritated me, like the fact that he was too needy and dependent on me for company. He tried to make contact with me almost every day, including the days immediately after Karen had joined him. Those two together indeed had a special relationship and spoke to one another in a personal patois that left me baffled, and finally disinterested. They always had plenty to talk about. Something funny had happened at work. They discoursed on a book one of them was reading. And they were full of questions. Did I have an opinion on this or that? How was the writing coming along? In truth, lot of the time they were amusing, but they were always exhausting.

One evening the apartment manager approached me in the dark hallway outside me room after work. I could tell he had bad news. "Tania died this morning," he said. He held a notepad and pen in his bent, arthritic hands. "I'm taking a collection for a wreath." I gave him a dollar and signed the notepad.

I remembered one Sunday afternoon when Tania knocked on my door. I opened the door and saw her standing there, frail, small, pale and frightened. She was holding her hand over her breasts, struggling with her breath. I had walked her back to her room and tried to comfort her. She sat on her narrow bed, in a room that was warm, cluttered, and dusty. It smelled of freshly cooked corned beef. Her television was tuned to a golf match. An open bible lay on a small night stand beside her rocker. A floor-to-ceiling ladder stood in front of tall bookshelves filled with books and coffee tins which she used to store her keepsakes and memories. Books lay scattered everywhere.

I went to the manager's apartment and called an ambulance because neither Tania nor I had a telephone. While the manager waited on the porch for the ambulance, I went back to Tania's room. Tania looked beautiful, completely conscious. Her color had already started to return. I gathered up some of her things as she asked me to; an envelope stuffed with money was hidden under a stack of records in the bottom drawer of her bureau. "I'm afraid I'm going to leave this earth," she said, trembling. I held her hand.

Tania tried to smile, despite her fear. She told me she was breathing better and that she felt embarrassed for making a fuss. "I feel stronger now," she murmured. "I know you do," I said, trusting it was true. "We'll do this just to be cautious, okay?" The ambulance arrived minutes later and the EMTs put Tania on a stretcher, strapping her down. She apologized over and over for causing a fuss, saying, "I don't want to be a nuisance."

Tania came home two days later, surprising Alex and me. We were expecting the worst, but Tania had us fooled. She asked me to help her fill out some Medicare papers and entertained Alex and me with an unrelenting flow of chatter. Her reprieve and quick recovery had energized her, giving her increased vigor and determination. She was telling so many stories that

I told Alex we ought to record her conversations. Alex disagreed, saying that would inhibit her. I believed she would have enjoyed every second of it. She was a romantic and an expert talker and she would have understood why I wanted to save her words. But I didn't.

On one occasion Alex and I watched her while she danced for us. She was exuberant, recalling her days as a professional dancer. She laughed and danced until Alex asked her to please slow down. She couldn't. After coming home she had quickly started her habitually rigorous schedule of activities. She spent a whole Saturday in the basement scrubbing rugs. She walked to the store every day and brought home heavy bags of groceries, more groceries than she needed because she was determined to cook huge meals which she demanded Alex and I eat. "Quit working so hard!" Alex cautioned her. "Please!"

On the last Sunday I talked to Tania she had been to church. She had read a message on a bulletin board. It said that one should attempt something unique every day as an expression of the desire to live a full life. Tania liked that. When I came home late that night I saw the ambulance parked in front of the house. Alex stood solemnly on the porch beside the manager. A first clutch of winter cooled the night air. In bedtime garb, Alex and the manager didn't seem to notice the chill. Their worried faces were blanketed by the flash of red and blue lights.

Apparently, Tania had knocked on Alex's door this time and the manager called the ambulance. I went to the ambulance's rear doors and peered in over the shoulder of an EMT. Tania was elevated slightly on the gurney. She wore an oxygen mask and her white hair glowed under the bright interior lights. I looked into her eyes. I thought I saw recognition, but I wasn't sure. Two weeks later I gave the manager a dollar for Tania's wreath.

The Long Goodbye

I eventually escaped the Everett Street flophouse and found a new place. I moved into a large studio apartment with a female co-worker from a restaurant where I had worked as a bus boy before landing the cooking position at the Kingston Tavern. Melanie was two years younger than me and worked as a waitress. She had vowed her love for me, as I did for her. Our love nest had hardwood floors, in an old, well-kept brick apartment building. It felt like paradise for a short time before reality once again landed a solid punch on my jaw.

Melanie, despite her avowed love for me, was still entangled with a high school senior in her home town of Newberg, a short drive from Portland. The kid was eighteen and she had been dating him for a number of years. Melanie was six-years older than her boyfriend, and I thought that was everything I needed to know about their relationship, which of course she told me was over. But of course that was not the truth. Shortly after we moved in together, Melanie started to see him again and it soon became apparent to me that her feelings for the fellow were not completely eradicated. I put up with it for too long, thinking I might win her devotion, which was an illusionary gambit from the start. Soon we had split up, except for the occasional glandular reprise at my new place. But I had already begun running with a new circle of friends with whom I began my quest for the writing life in earnest.

I met the poet David Sevedge, whose *nom de plume* was H. Home (Happy Home), in Carol Nebel's bookstore on 21st Avenue. I had written a puff piece about Carol's store for the *Northwest Neighbor* and so I had taken to visiting often. H. introduced himself and we became fast friends. I had recently started a literary supplement to the newspaper, which I called *Cold Eye*, borrowing a phrase from W.B. Yeats. H. submitted a poem that I liked a lot, so I published it. With that, my literary endeavor was off to a rousing start.

I soon began hanging out at a place on 23rd Avenue called the Breadline Café, sitting in the afternoons with H. and his wife Donita and others, including the writer and religious ascetic Mark Wilson, painter David Havlick, photographer Lee Santa, and assorted other artists who enjoyed the free flowing wine and beer and conversation that seemed to conjure out of cigarette smoke and thin air every afternoon. Before long a number of women other than Donita had joined the festivities and the relationships began to formulate in new and not so mysterious ways.

I met Callie at the Breadline through Wilson and we were soon living together in a large house on the southeast side of town with another friend, Mark Crawford. The relationship with Callie was even rockier than the earlier one with Melanie. It culminated in a near tragedy one night months after moving to the southeast side of town, when Callie, angry with her daughter, fell down a flight of steps with the two-year old. That neither of them broke their necks or any other bones seemed like an incredible miracle. We had of course been drinking. I took the event as a sign of things to come and ended the relationship, moving back to the northwest side.

It was with this sterling group of literati that I began visiting The Long Goodbye, a combined eatery and theater space in the warehouse district near the densely populated neighborhood where we all lived. The area would be given a fancy name in the 90s—the Pearl District—and turned into an upscale enclave of restaurants and condos at the edge of Portland's city center. But in 1977, it was a run-down district full of crumbling, turn-of-the-century warehouses where a few artists and craftsmen lived on a dime and a dream, satisfied with the inexpensive rent and plentiful solitude. At night, it was eerily dark and quiet, with long shadows, dim streetlights, and a foreboding noirish feel.

The café's owner, Richard Vidan, must have felt that vibe when he opened the place, naming it after Raymond Chandler's detective novel. The venue was a music, theater and poetry space in the enduring fashion of fifties and sixties New York and Berkeley coffee houses—a place where poets looked like poets. I haven't owned a beret in years, but I know I had a black one back then, and I'd usually don it for Tuesday night open mic, when the poets gathered. I carried my precious poems in a leather shoulder bag and kept a G harmonica in my tweed sports coat, just in case. At times I wore a beard or goatee to affect the Beat feel. The café was marked with genius, I knew, because I was among them. (Actually, I was too insecure to be a genius and wrote sub-par poetry to boot.) However, my friend Home really was a genius, and so was Mark Wilson. Walt Curtis, the unofficial poet laureate of the streets qualified, as did Katherine Dunn in the years before breaking out big-time with *Geek Love*, and John Shirley, the sci-fi writer. Shirley's energy shredded the café in the name of pure genius and ambition. Jay Rothbell, who married Shirley, before divorcing him and marrying Robert Sheckley, sometimes dropped by to read something funny and outrageous. And there were many others.

At times the aura of genius in the place kicked my ass. I didn't really belong there, except I enjoyed the scene because it was a hilarious entertainment. The aforementioned poetry supplement to the monthly newspaper I worked for at the time quoted Yeats' self-penned epitaph from *Under Ben Bulben:*

> *Cast a cold eye*
> *On life, on death.*
> *Horseman, pass by!*

The lyric always struck me as a righteous way to look at life and death—coldly. Not unfeelingly, but realistically. If one is fortunate enough to live for many years, what else is there? Celebrate and laugh at the end. Be as cold about death as life itself.

Editing the supplement, I managed to find a few poets at the café who gave me their work to publish. That's one reason I went there to begin with. I was looking for material. I assigned H. Home to score interviews with the poets. Home befriended Dunn and called his interview with her *Portrait of the Genius at 33*. He had read her books, *Truck* and *Attic*; I hadn't. He was the man for the job. The interview read like a kind of private joke from outer space, a couple of extraterrestrials shooting the breeze. It was vaguely comprehensible to most of my readership, but definitely a big score.

Walt Curtis was a favorite of mine on the scene. His friend
Marian Wheatley did an interview with him for the
supplement. Walt was a performance artist and made me
laugh uproariously, though many in the audience found him
unbearable. I haven't seen Walt much in the intervening
years, but in 1977 he was obscene and so determined to take
things so far over the edge that he became self-parodying,
which he knew. That was the point and he thrived on it.
Laughing at his own stuff, appalled by it seemingly, he
would break off a verse in mid-line and apologize for its lurid
nature—then plunge on, describing an enthralling moment of
homosexual love, or describing some other unspeakable act,
some other daunting emotion. "This is awful!" he'd shout,
protesting to himself like a member of his angry audience,
flailing his arms and running his fingers through his
deliberately unkempt hair before returning to his text and the
next outrage he had in store for everyone. Then
surprisingly—and not really surprisingly at all—Walt might
turn a perfectly stunning phrase—something that made
profound sense and transcended the vulgarity of his act.
Irrespective of their subject matter, his readings were always

theatrical, always about Walt throwing off convention. I liked the act. But not everyone did.

H. Home, for example, despised Walt's exaggerations. He stormed the stage one night, knocking Walt's mic over and shoving him to the floor. Home's hat flew off as he flailed at Walt, his shirt was ripped open, and he took Walt down and sat atop him and told Walt what he thought of his filthy art. Damn, that was a funny moment. My other good friend, Mark Wilson, hated Walt, too. He and Home just couldn't handle the assault on good taste that Walt provided every time he took the stage. But as I say, I found the scene hilarious, as much for my friends' reaction to it as for Walt's alleged sicknesses. Something in me simply wasn't adverse to people unleashing their peculiar demons on stage, or whatever else Walt may have been trying to accomplish.

My time in The Long Goodbye scene eventually dimmed and faded away. I left the monthly paper and ended the literary supplement, fathered my daughter, and went to work in the corporate world as a scriptwriter. I didn't miss the poetry scene at all, probably because I never really enjoyed reading my stuff out loud to begin with. I was always self-conscious and uncertain about my work. I realize something about poetry now. You tend to know it when you've done it right. I think in the months I went there I read three or four times— my voice just wasn't very strong and I knew it.

I haven't been to a poetry reading in years. These days I find them too stuffy and precious, which is probably how our scene in the seventies appeared to others. I don't think I'd have the patience to sit through one without knocking down the poets, as H. Home once did to Walt Curtis.

A Fraud in Paris

The year was 1979 and I had left my bartending job at the Goose Hollow Inn because I had once again been seized by the travel bug. This time, rather than return to New England or San Francisco, I decide to go to Europe. I'd saved a couple of grand by working hard at the bar and remaining frugal in a way I wasn't accustomed to and I bought a round trip ticket that was good for six months.

A six-month trip sounded fine to me. I threw a few things into my brother's reliable old Marine Corps duffel, bussed to Seattle, and boarded a 747 for a direct flight over Greenland to London's Heathrow Airport. The first leg of the trip was great. I stayed in London for two weeks, went out to Highgate to see Marx's grave, drank beer in the pubs (which closed too early and opened too late for my thirst), and spent a great deal of time in the British Museum.

I took the train to Aldeburgh, in Suffolk, northeast of London, where an arts and theater festival much like Ashland, Oregon's Shakespeare Festival is held every year. I was instantly captivated by the town, scenically resting at the confluence of the River Alde and the North Sea. Once an important port, Francis Drake's "Golden Hind" was built there. Drake, at the request of Elizabeth I, circumnavigated the world in the ship, in 1577-1580. But, unfortunately, the town's shipping commerce began to erode when savage coastal winds and tides regularly ripped the old port apart. In more recent times, Aldeburgh earned more fame by becoming the first British town to elect a female mayor—Elizabeth Garrett Anderson, in 1908.

Arriving in Aldeburgh in the off-season, I liked the town's slow pace. With its dearth of tourists it was a surprisingly inexpensive place to visit. I got a room for six-dollars a night overlooking the sea and hung out in a bar where each evening local musicians gathered and jammed on Scottish-Irish tunes and drank themselves into oblivion. I felt like I fit right in. But the best part of that side trip was getting there. I took the train, which uncoupled several cars in each city as it traveled toward the coast, a trip through increasingly wooded terrain and small villages sitting amidst beautiful landscapes of lush green foliage and open fields. By the time it pulled into Aldeburgh, one bright red car sat alone behind the engine. A young couple and an old man and I were the only riders left at the line's terminus at the waterfront.

In Notting Hill, the storied London neighborhood, I looked up a friend of a woman I was currently in love with. We had worked together at the Goose Hollow Inn. Jane, a British national married to an American, had encouraged me to fall for her in the pathetic way some married women encourage men to fall for them, out of a sense of unhappiness or unfinished dreams, or pure boredom. Then, not finding anything in me worthy of the abandonment of her husband, she cooled. We hadn't slept together, so our innocence was left intact. But my ego was smashed, which was merely another reason to make my trip to Europe a long one.

Jane's friend offered me something to eat and drink as I sat with her and her baby and made small talk. I wanted to tell her everything about my relationship with our mutual friend in Portland, but I held off. After awhile I began to sense that my visit was largely an effort to ingratiate myself into Jane's life. By being in her friend's London apartment I realized I was out-of-bounds, silly, obviously desperate. I left a short time later, having talked of nothing consequential. Waiting for the train later, I felt relieved that I hadn't acted the complete fool and talked too much about my love interest in Portland.

Unnerved by the visit to Notting Hill, I began to question why I was even in London. Had I gone simply to escape the harsh reality of my relationship with a married woman? It was over, and I was deeply upset by that fact, the unrequited aspect of love. And this is where my European adventure turned uncomfortable, even bizarre. Out of sorts now, fragmented by a barrage of conflicting emotions, I went to Paris, and, like a man afraid of his own shadow, I returned to London just as quickly as I'd left it.

Returning to London, the Calais customs officer examined my passport and clearly thought I might be smuggling contraband. In reality, I was in a state of utter confusion about what I wanted to do. On one hand I wanted to travel, on the other I wanted to return immediately to Portland and try to pick up the pieces of my relationship with Jane. I knew that was impossible, but I couldn't get her out of my mind. I felt incredibly unbalanced and lost. Rather than enjoy my trip and all the great potential it offered, I had fallen into a deep depression and a kind of cultural shock magnified by my brief misadventure in France. I was suddenly blanketed by a fog of indecision.

I'd crossed the channel from Dover and taken a train to Paris, where I sat down in a café near the Gare du Nord station and ordered a beer I didn't want. My mind raced, panic seized me, and I realized I had no place to go. I hadn't planned the trip; I'd left London impulsively and hadn't bothered to even book a room. I had no idea where the nearest inexpensive hotel was, or even if a room would be available should I find one. I looked around the bar. I approached several people, none of whom spoke English well enough to communicate— and I had no French. It occurred to me that my situation was desperate, with no place to go on a miniscule budget. A rich man might have climbed into a taxi and gone to the nearest expensive hotel and been unfazed. But I was certainly not rich; I was merely in a panic.

I went outside and looked around. The sun was going down and soon it would be dark. I had no idea where I was, having arrived completely unprepared. I was an innocent abroad. But that is not what I wanted to be. Still a young man, my head was filled with stories of Paris as seen through the eyes of Hemingway and Stein, Fitzgerald and Miller. Stories about and by them had filled my head with fantastic dreams. I probably knew the Lost Generation better than I knew my own generation for heaven's sake! I wanted to be like them. Drink like them. Talk like them. Write like them. I wanted to walk in their footsteps, live life as they had, as an expatriate moving effortlessly around the great city, exploring the neighborhoods, drinking in the cafes, talking rubbish with beautiful women. Hell, I would have even boxed a favorite poet to announce my literary arrival.

What a debacle! Instead of taxiing to a famous café I skulked back to the train station and bought a return ticket to

London. I wasn't frightened by London like I was Paris. I knew the London Underground by heart already. Moreover, I spoke English like everyone there. I had given up an eight-dollar a night room near the British Museum, where I'd looked greedily at Dickens' manuscripts under glass. And now I was unhinged in Paris. Sitting on the train to Calais I thought about my situation. Maybe I could find another deal in London. Maybe I could salvage my European sojourn and avoid further turmoil.

The customs officer looked at my passport. I'd crossed just hours earlier. He gave me a wondering gaze, lifted his brow in a manner that said: "What are you up to young man?" We both pondered that for a moment, but when I shrugged and said nothing, he allowed me to board the ferry and return to Dover.

In Paris, I had panicked. Why hadn't I bothered with French in high school and college? I cursed my poor education. Why hadn't I learned more about the physical layout of Paris? Why hadn't I done more research and planning? Surely people in London could have helped me. Though I was on a tight budget, someone might have steered me in the right direction if I had only opened my mouth and talked to people. If I had only been brave enough to say, "Help me, please."

I returned to Russell Square and the small hotel where I'd stayed in London, and I talked to the concierge about my old room. Had it been rented out? "No," the woman told me. "I'll take it then," I said, finally relaxing. The woman checked me in and smiled. I felt like she was laughing at me. I had told her I was going to Paris to write. Now even she knew what I knew. I was a fraud—a dreaming, love-lost, struggling fraud.

A short time later, I returned to the U.S. without writing anything in Europe worth keeping. I had blown the only opportunity I've ever had to go to Paris and walk the path of the Lost Generation. My dream had crumbled, turned to dust, and disappeared in a maze of confusion and despair. I've replayed that trip many times in my mind, and I turn out a fool every time.

The author, 1980; Lee Santa Photo

Terry Simons lives in Portland, Oregon. He
is the founder of Round Bend Press. His favorite
college football team is the Mighty Oregon
Ducks.

Write to: roundbendpress@yahoo.com

Follow his blog at:
roundbendpress.blogspot.com

Round Bend Press

Portland, Oregon

170

Notes

15125440R00105

Made in the USA
Middletown, DE
24 October 2014